CLUELESS ABOUT
cars

CLUELESS ABOUT

cars

AN EASY GUIDE TO
CAR MAINTENANCE AND REPAIR

LISA CHRISTENSEN

FIREFLY BOOKS

A FIREFLY BOOK

Published by Firefly Books (U.S) Inc. 2004

First printing

Publisher Cataloging-in-Publication Data (U.S.)

Christensen, Lisa, 1969–
   Clueless about cars : an easy guide to car maintenance and repair / Lisa Christensen.
[160] p. : ill., maps ; cm.
Includes bibliographical references and index.
Summary: Guide to dealing with general car maintenance and repairs, car emergencies and buying and selling a car.
ISBN: 1-55297-975-X (pbk.)
1. Automobiles–maintenance and repair. I. Title.
629.28'72 dc 22 TL152.C53 2004

Published in the United States in 2004 by
Firefly Books (U.S.) Inc.
P.O. Box 1338, Ellicott Station
Buffalo, New York 14205

Cover photograph: © LWA-Dann Tardif / Corbis / Magma
Illustrations: John Lightfoot
Electronic Formatting: Jean Lightfoot Peters

Printed in Canada

For the Saturday mechanic
in all of us.

Contents

Acknowledgments

So many faces swim before my eyes. So many people that said "go for it!" There are people in my life that have come and gone, but are not forgotten. You know who you are. To thank everyone who has helped me with this project would take another entire book, so I'll mention just a few.

First and foremost, let me thank Daniel J. Laxer—friend and colleague. Without you, "Daddy Dan," there probably would not have been a book. To Clare McKeon and Linda Pruessen, my editors at Key Porter Books—Clare for her limitless understanding and patience, and Linda for helping me get it done. To Barry and Promac Garage, for letting me haul scrap parts, for letting me continue to learning, and for helping me to never forget where I came from. To Simon Dufort, my personal trainer and friend, for understanding all those missed sessions. To Charles and Murray—friends forever. To Dino and Joe of the law firm Lapointe Rosenstein. To Rheal and Patrick, "the guys" at work. And to "Tap," for showing me the light. To George Iny and Mathiew St. Pierre of the Automobile Protection Association in Montreal for all the great information. To Merson Automotive. To the Ford Motor Co. in Montreal.

And to Vito, thank you for not putting on the brakes.

Introduction: Your Car Will Thank You

Do you hear that little voice whispering "thank you, thank you, thank you" in your ear? That's your car, and it's extremely grateful that you've not only taken the time to find this book, but that you've also bothered to plunk down some of your hard-earned money to buy it. That fact that you *have* bothered to do this suggests that you're just the sort of person who should own a car—a caring person, a thoughtful person, a person who takes his or her investment seriously.

Yup, I said "investment." Because whatever else your car may be—a statement of independence, a symbol of your social status or financial success, a way to get from Point A to Point B without walking—it also represents an investment of your money. For most of us, cars rank second only to houses in terms of major life expenses. And, unlike houses, cars don't appreciate in value. These days, new cars cost anything from $15,000 to upwards of $300,000, depending on what you're buying. That's a lot of cash.

What does any of this have to do with a book on car maintenance and repair? It's simple, really. If you've recently plunked down $30,000 on a new set of wheels, don't you owe it to yourself to ensure that you get the most mileage—figuratively and literally—out of your investment? Cars may not appreciate in value, but they can and do depreciate at different rates. This means that the better you look after your baby, the longer your baby will stick around, which means that you're putting some welcome distance between yourself and the next occasion on which you'll have to part with $30,000. And that can only be good news, right?

So, by purchasing this book, you've made a commitment to yourself and to your car. You deserve a pat on the back!

What's Inside?

In the pages that follow, you'll find a wealth of information on caring for your car. It doesn't matter if you're new to the car game, or if you're a seasoned pro. It doesn't matter if you know the difference between a brake pedal and a brake pad. This book has been written in a way that anyone—even the most uninformed or "clueless" automotive consumer—can understand.

In the first few chapters, you'll become acquainted with some of your car's fundamental systems and features. If you've ever wondered what a camshaft is, or felt your eyes glaze over when your mechanic started talking about pistons and valves, you'd better not skip this part. Knowledge is the key to power, and you'll be a lot more powerful as a consumer once you finish this part of the book. You'll also learn the basics of preventive maintenance—do you have *any* idea how many fluids and filters your car needs in order to run efficiently? If not, you will!—and about how to make a preliminary diagnosis when something goes wrong.

When things do go wrong (and believe me, they will) you've got two choices: take your baby to a garage, or attempt to fix it yourself. I'll tell you when it's safe to try something yourself, and when you absolutely need a mechanic on the job. Your relationship with your mechanic is kind of like the relationship you have with your hairdresser: when it's good, it's very, very good, and when it's bad, it's awful. How do you find someone you like and trust? I'll help you figure it out. I'll also help you to communicate effectively with your new best friend. If you can't clearly explain what's wrong with your car, your chances of getting it fixed decrease dramatically. In Chapter 4, Diagnosing Your Car's Symptoms, we'll cover the basics of "mechanic-speak," including the difference between a tic and a toc, a bang and a knock, and a chirp and a creak. Don't laugh… this stuff does actually matter!

If you decide to tackle a minor repair or maintenance task yourself, never fear. Chapter 6, Gettin' Down and Dirty: Lisa's Do-It-Yourself Guide, tells you what you need to know about oil changes, the installation of new wiper blades and even the protocol for a proper car wash. Rounding things off are chapters on dealing with emergencies (including what you should have on hand in case of a breakdown), your car and the environment and buying and selling a vehicle. A Resource section and a comprehensive glossary of car terms are also included.

Your relationship with your car should be a long and happy one. I hope that *Clueless About Cars* will help make this possible for you.

—Lisa Christensen, 2004

Getting to Know Your Car

Most of us can tell a fan belt from a cinch belt or a spark plug from a hair plug. But would you know what to do if your timing chain suddenly snapped in the middle of nowhere? Do you feel like you're being hosed when your mechanic talks to you about, well, hoses, ballast resistors, differentials and drive shafts? Consider this volume a self-help book for car owners. After reading it, you should be able to pull into your local garage, head held high, brimming with automotive confidence. You may even be able to avoid the garage altogether and try some basic repairs yourself. Who hasn't wanted to tinker under the hood at some point? This book will be a welcome companion for those times when you can't get to your local garage, or when you want to save a few bucks and get your hands dirty.

A Healthy Car Is a Happy Car

Even a new car will break down if it's not looked after. Your car's got hundreds of moving parts that start to wear down the minute you drive it off the lot. Did you know that as soon as you leave the dealership the value of your new purchase decreases substantially, by approximately 25 percent? Even though proper maintenance and driving technique will extend the life of your car and its parts, wear-out and breakdown are only a matter of time. A car owner must think like a Boy Scout: be prepared, and make sure you've got the necessary tools. We'll talk about what that means in the next few chapters.

Poetry in perpetual motion

You may have heard the expression "poetry in motion." Indeed, car talk is peppered with metaphors. A car has a body. You take care of your own body by feeding it the right foods, and making sure it's clean and in good working order. You see a doctor when part of you breaks down, but if you eat right and take care of yourself, you avoid breakdown and need to see the doctor only once a year for a checkup.

Do unto your car as you would do unto yourself. Or to paraphrase the immortal Socrates, know thy car. If you've got a new car, read through the owner's manual. If you've got a used car (secondhand, pre-owned, whatever; if someone had it before you, it's used), there are several resources for information on the model, make, and year of your car (see Resources).

Understanding the symptom before a part actually breaks down will not only save you money, it can also save your life. We'll get into safety tips in subsequent sections—this is important stuff. For now, let's get into the basic makeup of your car. Did you think of the vanity mirror when I said "makeup"? Well, that's not what I meant. I'm talking about your car's components.

The Engine

We've come a long way since the first Model T rolled off Ford's assembly line, but the basic principles of a car's **engine** have remained unchanged for about 100 years. The engine is your car's nerve center, complete with little synaptic explosions that keep your car's heart and lungs pumping and sending messages to all the other components, resulting in movement.

We've Come a Long Way, Baby

In 1769, French engineer and mechanic Nicolas Cugnot invented the first self-propelled road vehicle—a steam-powered military tractor that hauled artillery at a breakneck speed of 2.5 mph (4 km/h)—on three wheels, no less! It took more than 100 years of trial and error before Nicolaus Otto finally invented an effective gas motor engine in 1876. Dubbed the Otto Cycle Engine, it was the first practical four-stroke internal combustion engine. Nine years later, a few important things happened: Karl Benz designed and built the world's first automobile to be powered by an internal combustion engine, and Gottlieb Daimler and Wilhelm Maybach patented what is now recognized as the prototype of the modern gas engine. The automotive era was officially under way.

Building blocks and engine blocks

The ad slogan for one of the first cars read "Dispense with the horse." For a long time an automobile (meaning "self-moving") was called a horseless carriage. The horses had been replaced by the internal combustion engine. Well, not right away. The steam engine came first, with the first cars bearing more resemblance to a horseless carriage, using the same system of levers to steer and stop the car. We still talk in terms of horsepower, a term that basically refers to engine performance. Horsepower measures how hard your engine needs to work to lift 550 pounds (250 kg) one foot (30 cm) in one second.

Looking under the hood of your car can sometimes make you feel like a blockhead. But it's the engine that's the blockhead: a car engine is made up of two basic parts, the **engine block** and the **engine head**, each of which has a few basic components. The engine block has pistons, gears, a crankshaft, one or more camshafts (which, depending on the model, might be part of the engine head) and a timing chain or belt. The engine

The Internal Combustion Engine

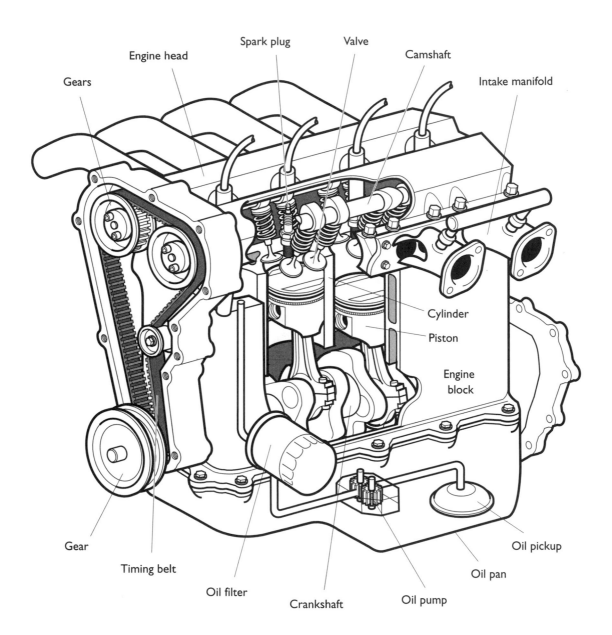

Gears

Engine head

Spark plug

Valve

Camshaft

Intake manifold

Cylinder

Piston

Engine block

Gear

Timing belt

Oil filter

Crankshaft

Oil pump

Oil pan

Oil pickup

head consists of the cylinder head, valves, perhaps a camshaft, a carburetor or a fuel injector (mostly in newer models), as well as spark plugs (which will need changing every so often) and assorted springs, seals and gaskets.

"I could have had a V-8"

There are various types of engines, from the in-line 4-cylinder type to the V-8, which is an 8-cylinder engine with the cylinders aligned in a V formation. But all car engines are internal combusion engines. What does that mean? It means that you're driving a bomb. The energy that gets your car moving derives from a tiny explosion that occurs when an electric spark ignites the gasoline vapor that's formed inside the engine. The **cylinder block**, your engine's spine, holds the cylinders, where the explosions happen. A **piston** slides up a cylinder, compressing a concoction of gasoline and air toward the top, to what's called the combustion chamber, where the **spark plug** ignites the gasoline vapor and BANG! The explosion pushes the piston back down the cylinder. Multiply this movement by the number of cylinders, and voila, you have a rotating crankshaft. It's this combination of movement—a conversion of chemical energy into mechanical energy, timed just right—that results in the rotary power needed to get your car going.

Then there are the **valves**. These are your car's lungs. As a human, you need to breathe right when you exercise: in with the good air, out with the bad. It's the same thing with a car. The **camshaft** opens and closes the valves at the right times, one valve to let in air and fuel, the other to let out exhaust. On some cars, the camshaft is part of the engine block. On others, it's part of the head (called an overhead camshaft). Different engine types have different combinations of cylinders and valves. A basic V-8 with two valves per cylinder is a 16-valve engine. A 4-cylinder engine with three valves per cylinder is, of course, a 12-valve engine. (Refer to your owner's manual to see how many valves your engine has.)

When it comes to opening and closing valves, timing is everything. That and getting just the right mixture of fuel and air into the combustion process.

The Transmission

You already know, I'm sure, that a transmission can either be standard or automatic. But what exactly is your car's transmission, and what does it do? The transmission makes the car move. "But wait a minute," you say, "didn't I just read that the engine is what gets the car moving?" Well, yes, because the engine is your car's source of power—and so is the battery. But without the transmission, you won't move. Confused? Read on.

Your car's transmission harnesses power from the engine—what we call the turning force or torque—and transmits it to the axles and the wheels, setting the car in motion. Again, think of your car in terms of your own body. Just as nerves carry messages from the brain to the other parts of your body, the transmission carries power from the engine to the moving parts: the axles and the wheels.

Sometimes a stick shift is just a stick shift

The basic difference between standard (or manual) and automatic transmission systems is that the standard transmission uses a stick shift and clutch to change gears, while the automatic transmission uses hydraulic pressure. The transmission's other basic components include the torque converter, valve body, clutches, bands, gears, teeth, fluid (transmission oil), a filter and assorted other bits and pieces.

The **clutch** engages and disengages the engine from the transmission, basically putting your car in neutral so that you can switch gears smoothly. With a stick shift that takes some practice; if you're new to standard driving, you'll probably pop the clutch, jerking yourself and your passengers around. Best not have anything in your beverage holder while you're learning!

Most standard cars come with a 5-speed transmission, the fifth gear being an overdrive normally used only for highway driving. A **tachometer** tells you when to shift from one gear to another, according to your engine's revolutions per minute (RPMs or "revs"). Some drivers, however, prefer to use engine sounds as a gauge.

Be gentle on your transmission. Jamming the car into park or reverse before you've come to a complete stop is hard on the transmission, to say the least, as is skipping gears and driving in the wrong gear, which could cause the transmission to over-heat. If you're ever stuck in snow or mud, keep in mind that spinning your wheels can also cause the transmission to overheat.

The Suspension

When you drive over speed bumps, potholes and dirt roads, your car and the people in it are taking quite a beating. But most of the time it's a pretty comfortable ride. That's because your car is suspended in mid-air. Okay, not exactly, but the body is certainly held or cradled, as it were, in a kind of buffer zone called the suspension, which comprises a series of coil springs and shock absorbers, or shock absorber spring assem-blies called MacPherson struts. Each car has both a front-end suspension and a rear-end suspension. Together, they keep the car stable.

The Steering

A clever automotive columnist might call his weekly feature "The Steering Column," named for one of the three main com-ponents of a car's steering system: the **steering column**, the **steering linkage** and the **steering gear**. The steering wheel is considered part of the column.

These days, most cars are equipped with a **rack-and-pinion steering system**. A pinion is a gear that connects the steering column to a toothed rack. When you turn the steering wheel, the pinion moves the rack back and forth. The rest of the steer-ing linkage turns the front wheels either left or right.

Before the advent of power steering, driving was a great way to build up your arm muscles; parallel parking was almost as

The Rack-and-Pinion Steering System

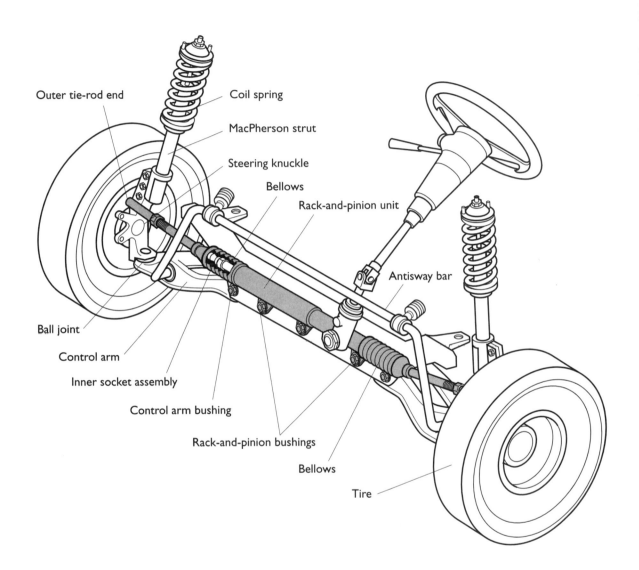

Outer tie-rod end

Coil spring

MacPherson strut

Steering knuckle

Bellows

Rack-and-pinion unit

Ball joint

Control arm

Inner socket assembly

Control arm bushing

Rack-and-pinion bushings

Antisway bar

Bellows

Tire

good a workout as arm curls or push-ups. But it led to driver fatigue and wasn't very safe. Power steering uses hydraulics— the use of fluid to set mechanical parts in motion—to make steering easier on the arms.

The Brakes

"How do you make a car top?" goes an old children's riddle. "You 'tep on the brake, 'tupid."

The brakes slow and stop the car using a system of fluids, hydraulics and friction. When you push down on the brake pedal, you're compressing hydraulic fluid, which pushes out pistons, which in turn push brake friction material into contact with either discs (in the front) or drums (in the back). (For a more detailed discussion of your car's braking system, see Chapter 3.) After a while, your brakes will wear down and will have to be replaced. Like horses—and like you and me—your car needs a new pair of shoes now and again. Your mechanic may also tell you that you're low on brake fluid. We'll discuss that further in Chapter 2, when we dip into all the fluids sloshing around inside your car.

Slippery road conditions sometimes render your brakes useless. If you've driven in wintry weather, you've no doubt known the panic of barreling toward the driver in front of you

Faster than a Speeding Bullet

ABS brakes are not a substitute for good judgment. In slippery weather, keep in mind that you need to leave more space in front of you and start breaking sooner than you normally do. Your car is a speeding bullet that could do serious damage. Bear that in mind, and keep your distance.

no matter how hard you press on the brakes. An **antilock brake system (ABS)** takes some of the pressure off. When you push hard on the brake pedal, a computer opens and closes a valve rapidly, controlling the amount of fluid that operates the brake. This prevents lockup, and what mechanics call "slip," giving the car better control.

The Tires

Good **tires** will keep your car on the road, and will help when it comes to slowing down and stopping. Since only a hand-sized section of rubber touches the road at any given time, you need to have good tires, and they need to be the right ones for specific driving conditions. All-seasons won't do in the winter; spend the extra money on snow tires for safety's sake.

Tire manufacturers go to the trouble of writing important information on the wall of your tires. In Chapter 3, we'll get into what it all means, as well as proper tire maintenance and things like air pressure and when to check it.

The Body

You're clean, right? You no doubt bathe regularly, maybe even use cosmetics to hide that bit of gray in your beard or to touch up your face. And you chose your car because of its style, color and so forth, didn't you? It really is an extension of you. It's important to protect your investment, to keep your car's body beautiful. You'd be surprised by how important a proper paint job is to your car's aerodynamic performance; chips, rust and rough edges slow a body down. Keep it looking good, clean and free of rust. And don't be fooled, by the way, by plastic cars such as the Saturn. There's still a lot of metal in there, and it needs to be kept up.

The Electrical System

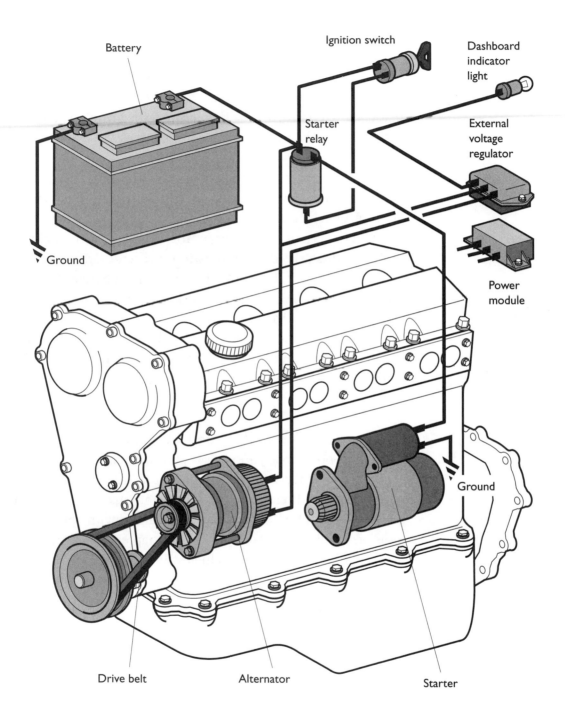

Battery

Ignition switch

Dashboard indicator light

Starter relay

External voltage regulator

Ground

Power module

Ground

Drive belt

Alternator

Starter

The Electrical System

Like that annoying pink bunny on TV, your car keeps on going and going—as long as you pump it full of gas and all the necessary fluids. But there's an electrical system in there, too, and you can't take that for granted. Think of all the components that need electricity to run: the lighting, the horn, power accessories such as the radio and power antennae, the trunk release, electric door locks and windows, and so on.

Your car's electrical system consists of the **battery**, the **alternator** and the **starter motor**. When you turn the key, the ignition switch causes an electrical chain reaction. Power from the battery goes to the starter motor, which in turn cranks the motor and starts the combustion process. The alternator replaces the power that you've taken from the battery to power up the car and the stuff in it. But don't think of it as a battery charger. It's more like a generator.

Fixing a problem with the electrical system might be a simple matter of changing a fuse. However, I'll help you decide when it's time to take the car into the shop.

That's a basic guide to what's under your hood. Now clear out your glove box. Once you pay off all those parking tickets and learn how to properly fold up your maps, you'll find you've got more space in there than you thought, maybe even room enough for this book. Toss it in there, along with some of the tools we'll talk about in the next few chapters. It's time to roll up your sleeves. You may be clueless now, but by the time you reach the end of this book you might actually be able to tell your mechanic a thing or two.

2

Protecting Your Investment: Preventive Maintenance

As a mechanic, I sometimes wish I could have car owners charged with neglect. Don't worry, though. No matter how delinquent you may be in the upkeep of your car, no one will take your baby away. But if you try to think about your car as a baby, you may begin to see how important it is to take care of it, and maybe even pamper it once in a while. Otherwise, you're throwing money away.

Your car needs you just as much as you need it. There are certain things you should to do to ensure it is maintained properly. Your car needs a regular physical checkup, just as you or your children do. But taking care of your car can be a simple matter; you don't have to splurge on a whole case of protect-all cleaner, just follow your dealer's regular maintenance schedule. It's right there in the owner's manual, which—after you've read it through—you should keep in the glove box along with this book. But too many drivers just leave their manual in the glove box and don't consult it until something goes wrong. This chapter is all about prevention. The more you know about your car, the better you'll be at preventing problems.

In this chapter I'll provide a detailed list of everything you need to do to keep your car alive and kicking: replacing the oil and all the other mystery fluids that flow through your car, including gasoline; changing filters; and, of course, taking your baby in for a tune-up.

Going with the Flow

There are many fluids that flow through your car, all of which are what we call maintenance items, which means they all need to be changed or topped up regularly. You'll notice changes in your car's performance if any of these fluids are not maintained properly, so it'll help you if you know a little about each one.

Engine oil

Oil is the lifeblood of your car, and it needs to be checked and changed regularly. Just as blood flows to and from the heart through a complex network of veins and arteries, so your engine oil flows through the nooks, crannies, cracks and crevices built into your car's engine. If your lubrication is not properly maintained, your car can suffer what is tantamount to clogged arteries. Unchecked and unchanged, motor oil gets mucked up with dirt and can wear down your car's mechanical parts. It thickens—a process called viscosity breakdown—and won't flow the way it should. Having your engine flushed out can be a costly pain in the butt. It makes much more sense to prevent the problem from arising in the first place.

Oil has four main purposes. First, and quite fundamentally, oil *lubricates*—reducing friction between all of your engine's moving parts, preventing wear and tear, or at least prolonging the life of your engine. At the same time, oil acts as a liquid gasket. It *seals* certain key areas, like the minuscule space between the pistons and the cylinder walls. When dirt that gets into those tiny areas, it breaks the seal and can cause leakage. So the oil also *cleans* those spaces as it lubricates and seals, flushing out collected detritus like dirt, rust and carbon, and carrying it to the oil filter.

While all of this is going on, your engine and its parts are getting hot. As the oil flows through the engine, it *cools*, absorbing heat and carrying it away from each part. This is important: if you don't have the right amount of good, clean oil in your car, your engine can overheat. Coolant works the same way, as you'll see further on.

Synthetic Oils

In addition to the regular motor oils that you can buy for your car, a number of good synthetic oils are now available. Although synthetic products are also made from mineral oil, the oil itself is more refined—meaning that its molecules have been manipulated to increase performance. Synthetic motor oils can be designed to run well at low temperatures or high temperatures, and they tend to last longer than regular motor oils. They are also more expensive.

Your engine's lubrication system is much like your own circulatory system, with one organ that pumps oil through your car (just as your heart pumps blood) and another that cleans the oil as much as possible (just as your kidneys purify blood). Here's how it works: Most cars can take up to 1.5 gallons (5 l) of oil. When you pour the oil into the engine, it flows down into the **oil pan** at the bottom, where it sits until you start your car. That's also where it settles after you turn your car off. When you start your car, the **oil pump** (heart) draws oil from the pan up through the **oil filter** (kidneys), where it's cleaned, and then into the engine, where it flows through all of your engine's nooks and crannies. Once the oil reaches the top of the engine, having lubricated, sealed, cleaned and cooled all of its parts, it drips back down into the pan.

With so many mechanical parts, cogs and gears rubbing against each other and causing friction, simply driving your car causes damage. Most of this damage happens on start-up. We mechanics say that a cold car—one that's been sitting in your driveway all night—starts up dry. Even though there is a bit of oil residue in the engine's nooks and crannies from the last

The Lubrication System

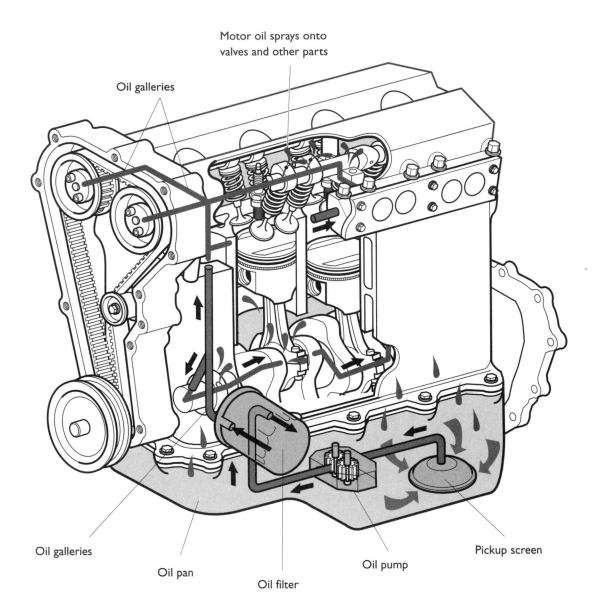

Motor oil sprays onto valves and other parts

Oil galleries

Oil galleries

Oil pan

Oil filter

Oil pump

Pickup screen

time you drove it, the bulk of the oil is sitting in the oil pan. When you crank your engine, turning the key until the car starts, you're wearing your engine down—that is, until the oil actually starts flowing. That's why you need your oil to flow well, especially in severe driving conditions. Have you ever tried to pour molasses from the carton right out of the fridge?

That's what severe cold does to oil. When the engine sputters to life, you want to make sure you have the right oil in your car for the right kind of weather.

Oil gets used up, so you need to top it up every so often. A gas attendant might offer to check your oil for you, and the honest ones will tell you if you've got enough. But if you know how to check the oil yourself, you can do it regularly and avoid problems.

You should have your oil changed completely, along with the oil filter, every three months or 3,000 miles (5,000 km), whichever comes first. But that could vary depending on driving conditions and the kind of driving you do, and, of course, on your dealer's recommendations. It's always a good idea to check your owner's manual. Changing the oil is something you can do by yourself, if you are so inclined. I'll teach you how in Chapter 6.

If your car is a recent model, it may have an **oil minder light** that will tell you when it's time to change the oil. Your car's computer takes into account factors such as temperature, mileage and speed, so you could go 4,500 miles (7,000 km) without the light coming on. And some dealers still keep tabs on their customers, giving them a friendly call when it's time for an oil change, at least according to the dealer's schedule.

As I said in Chapter 1, it's important to know and understand your car. If this relationship is going to work, you're going to have to become a good listener. If you know your car well enough, you'll be able to tell on your own when it's time to change the oil. I'll go into more detail about this in Chapter 6.

Antifreeze

They say that the sidewalks in Arizona can get hot enough to fry an egg. Well, so can your engine. In fact, Chris Maynard and Bill Scheller have created a book of recipes that can be cooked right there under your hood on the engine manifold. *Manifold Destiny: The One, the Only Guide to Cooking on Your Car Engine!* says that what you prepare for dinner depends on your destination: the farther you drive, the hotter your car gets.

That is, until the cooling system kicks in. Remember that your engine works on combustion. There is fire under the

Lisa's Tip
If you don't change your oil as often as your manufacturer recommends, you run the risk of voiding your vehicle warranty. If you prefer to do oil changes yourself, make sure to purchase the correct filter, use the recommended grade of oil, note the mileage and date and keep all of your receipts as a record.

The Cooling System

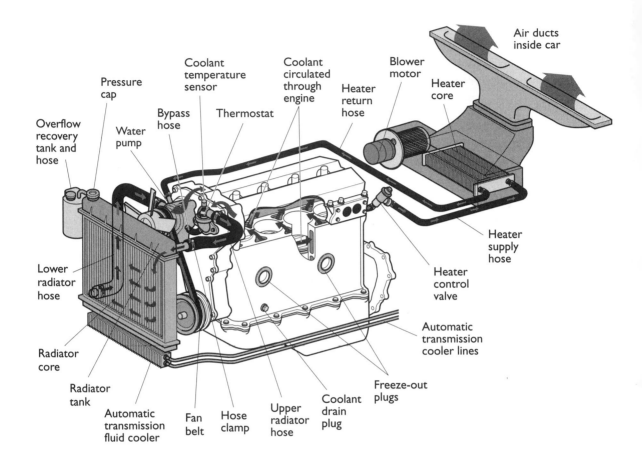

Air ducts inside car

Coolant temperature sensor

Coolant circulated through engine

Blower motor

Heater core

Pressure cap

Bypass hose

Heater return hose

Thermostat

Overflow recovery tank and hose

Water pump

Heater supply hose

Lower radiator hose

Heater control valve

Automatic transmission cooler lines

Radiator core

Radiator tank

Freeze-out plugs

Automatic transmission fluid cooler

Fan belt

Hose clamp

Upper radiator hose

Coolant drain plug

hood, and at times your engine can get hot enough to boil water, or even hotter, sometimes reaching temperatures of up to 2,500°F (1,371°C)! That kind of heat can really damage your car, so it's important to keep it controlled. Your healthy body temperature is 98.6°F (37°C). If it goes above that, you've got a fever and don't function as well as you should. Your car also won't function if it gets too hot. The cooling system keeps the engine at its most efficient operating temperature at all speeds and in all driving conditions. In other words, despite its name, the cooling system's purpose is not to keep the engine cool, but to keep it from getting too hot.

The cooling system runs on antifreeze. By the way, "coolant" and "antifreeze" both refer to the same product. We don't try to confuse you on purpose. Honest! Call it a flaw in the lingo. It may say antifreeze on the bottle, but mechanics call it coolant. It's the same thing. Antifreeze can be either ethylene-glycol, which is green, or propylene-glycol, which is pink. I'll explain the difference between the two a bit farther on. For now, let's talk about how the cooling system actually works.

Your coolant does not go into the car at full strength, but should be diluted, combining 50 percent antifreeze with 50 percent water. This mixture flows through the cooling system, controlling the engine's temperature through heat exchange, absorbing heat from one place and carrying it away to another. Just as your lubrication system uses a pump to get the oil flowing through the engine, so the cooling system uses a **water pump** to get the coolant flowing. The coolant flows through the cylinder block and head, through a thermostat, and into the radiator. The **radiator fan** draws air in from the outside. This is where the heat exchange takes place. The liquid conducts the heat into the air, and the air, in turn, cools the liquid, which moves on, back to its starting point in the water pump to get recirculated into the engine. The liquid does not always have to be cooled, though. The thermostat might decide that the liquid is still cool enough to bypass the radiator and go right back to the pump for recirculation. If that's the case, the passage to the radiator is closed off, redirecting the coolant into the water pump.

Antifreeze maintains itself. It's made with additives that help prevent corrosion and other problems. But the additives do eventually break down. Like engine oil, antifreeze needs to be changed regularly. Ethylene-glycol, the green stuff, should be changed every two years or 25,000 miles (40,000 km). Propylene-glycol, which is newer, is considered long-life antifreeze.

Unlike changing your oil, changing coolant is not a do-it-yourself job. It can be very dangerous if you don't know what you're doing. The heat, along with the pressure that builds up in the system, can lead to liquid exploding from the radiator. Even the most seasoned mechanic is susceptible to severe burns to the face if she's not careful.

Lack of heat in the winter or overheating in the summer

could indicate a leak in the cooling system. Either problem might indicate that your coolant needs to be changed. If you suspect your coolant is leaking, take the car to the garage.

The **radiator cap** is an important component of the cooling system, by the way. It has valves that, under certain pressure, will give way and allow some coolant into a reservoir or the overflow area. Once the pressure decreases, the radiator cap allows the coolant back into the system.

Brake fluid

Your brake system is also known as a **hydraulic brake system**. Translated into English, this means that the system uses liquid to stop the car or to slow it down. The fluid, of course, is hydraulic brake fluid. When you step on the brake pedal, you're pushing brake fluid through the brake lines. In turn, this liquid pushes against the mechanism that actually slows down or stops the car. This works because, unlike a gas, a liquid cannot be compressed. If you push it, it moves, like a mechanical part.

It's important to note that brake fluid is not oil. It's a specially blended hydraulic liquid that has a big responsibility. It must be compatible with all the materials used in the components of your brake system. Like motor oil, your brake fluid lubricates, so mechanics talk about brake fluid in terms of its proper viscosity: it must not be too thick or thin, but should be just the right quality at all times. It must withstand heat, so that it doesn't evaporate at high temperatures. At the same time, it must not freeze. And it has to be water tolerant, so that any water that gets into the system won't cause problems.

Again, brake fluid is a maintenance item, so it needs to be replaced regularly (generally every couple of years, but check your owner's manual). If you're not sure, you can't go wrong if you change it every two years.

Brake fluid can leak. If you're low on brake fluid, your brakes will feel soft, and you'll find you need more distance, and more pressure from your foot, to stop your car. That can be disastrous if the car in front of you stops suddenly. If you suspect you have a leak, have your brakes checked. But *do not* top up your brake fluid yourself unless it's an emergency. Here's

Lisa's Tip

If you're in the habit of keeping brake fluid on hand in case of emergencies, remember that it has a shelf life of one month. Keep it in a sealed container and label it so you know when it was purchased. Once opened, it has a shelf life of one month.

why: When your mechanic checks your brakes, she applies pressure to the system. If you've added liquid to the system, it will overflow. If you do have to add fluid in an emergency situation, let your mechanic know. And never add any liquid to brake fluid except water. As I said, brake fluid is compatible with water, and that will get you through until you get to a garage to have the brakes checked.

Power-steering fluid

Like the brake system, your steering system is likely hydraulic. (There aren't too many cars on the road these days that do not have at least some kind of power-steering system.) The steering system uses a special fluid that applies pressure to the steering gear when you turn the wheel. In an emergency situation, a little transmission fluid can be tossed in to keep the fluid level up, but normally only the power-steering fluid is needed. If you need to add transmission fluid to get you to a garage, let the mechanic know, and she will flush out the system and check it.

The next chapter, on driver safety, will go into more detail about the steering system.

Transmission oil

You need a bit of oil flowing through your transmission to cool and lubricate its components, such as the **transfer case** and the **differential**, which transfer rotary power from the engine to the wheels. Depending on your car, you need either motor oil, gear oil or automatic transmission fluid. And, like the other fluids, transmission oil is a scheduled maintenance item: it needs to be checked and changed regularly by a mechanic.

Gasoline

Back in the dark ages, gasoline contained lead. Now, thanks to our more environmentally conscious ways, all gasoline is unleaded. But not all gasoline is created equal. In fact, gasoline quality may vary from gas station to gas station. That largely comes down to marketing, with some stations promising a "clean" gasoline, and others saying they put special additives in their product to make it better for your car. If you are an attentive car owner with the kind of savvy I hope I'm imparting, you

Lisa's Tip

Got an unidentified leak? Try putting a piece of cardboard on the driveway under you car to catch the leaking fluid. (Old pizza boxes work well, especially if they are white.) It can help you isolate the location of the leak, and the type of fluid that's leaking. Make note of the fluid's color and pass the information on to your mechanic.

Get the Lead Out

Until the early 1970s, most cars ran on leaded gasoline. By the mid-1970s, growing concern over the health effects of lead emissions fostered a gradual phasing out of lead in gasoline. In the United States, the *Clean Air Act* now prohibits the introduction of gasoline containing lead or lead additives into commerce for use as a motor vehicle fuel. Many other countries have followed suit.

just might notice a difference in your car's performance depending on where you purchase your gas.

Gasoline is a petroleum-based product. Like all oil products, it starts off as crude, and gets refined into the go-juice that sets your car in motion. There are two or three different kinds, or grades, of gasoline, ranging from regular to super or supreme. "Super" gasoline is a higher-octane gasoline. Octane itself is not a substance, although when you hear a gas attendant use the term it may sound like she's talking about an additive—almost as if putting something called octane into your gas line will give your car an energy boost. That's not the case. Octane is not a vitamin for your car. "High octane" refers to a gasoline's "octane number," which rates the gasoline's ability to reduce knocking or pinging in the internal combustion engine. The recommended gasoline for most cars is regular octane. In most cases, using a higher-octane gasoline offers no benefit. It won't make your car go better, run cleaner or get better mileage.

Higher-performance engines, on the other hand, need a higher-octane gasoline because they use more compression. Your owner's manual will tell you what grade of gasoline your car needs, or you can check the inside of the gas cap. Gasoline may also contain detergents, gas-line antifreeze and other additives to help keep your engine clean and in working order. We'll talk a bit more about that in Chapter 8, as anything that burns in your car will end up in the air we breathe.

Fuel injection was once the latest technology. Now it's commonplace. Most modern cars use gasoline injection to get an even mixture of gasoline and air to form the gasoline vapor needed to run an internal combustion engine. That used to be the carburetor's job, but it was never a perfect system: the amount of gasoline vapor was never exact. Fuel injection evens things out. While air is still being drawn in through what's called the **carburetor body**, an exact amount of gasoline is injected into each individual cylinder. The resulting mixture is more economical, better performing and more environmentally friendly.

Checklist Your Car's Fluids

Here's a basic checklist of your car's fluids. Use it to work your way through your owner's manual, and make notes about how often these fluids need to be replaced.

- ✔ Brake fluid
- ✔ Differential fluid
- ✔ Engine coolant
- ✔ Engine oil
- ✔ Power-steering fluid
- ✔ Transfer case fluid
- ✔ Transmission fluid
- ✔ Windshield washer fluid

Filters

There are several filters in your car, filtering air or fluid. All of them need to be changed regularly. A quick word about each.

The air needed for the combustion process comes into the car through the air induction system. Bits of dirt and sand are abrasive to the cylinder, causing tiny nicks and scratches that compromise the combustion process. The **air filter** helps to prevent debris from getting in. Air filters are available in different qualities and are generally made from paper and fibers. The better ones can last two to three years, while a cheaper one might last only until your next oil change.

Dirt and other particles, like rust and stray carbon, can be siphoned into the engine from the gas tank, and could damage the engine. The **gas filter** strains dirt out before it gets there. Older gas filters had to be changed once a year. These days, your gas filter could last up to 35,000 miles (60,000 km) or more, depending on the manufacturer.

When you open the vent in your car, you're breathing in air that gets sucked in from the outside—air and all the detritus that comes with it. The **cabin filter** or **pollen filter** helps to clean the air that goes into the cabin, which, like on an airplane, is where you and your family sit. Driving conditions will dictate when the filter should be changed. For example, if you regularly drive on dirt roads or in slushy conditions, you may have to change your filter sooner than your manufacturer recommends.

Transmission fluid also gets cleaned through a filtration system. Your car might have either a **transmission filter** or a simple screen through which the liquid flows. The screen doesn't need to be changed. When your mechanic services your transmission, she might simply remove the screen, clean it and put it back.

Checklist Your Car's Filters

Use this list to guide you through your owner's manual. It will offer suggestions on how often your filters need to be replaced.

- ✔ Air filter
- ✔ Cabin (or pollen) filter
- ✔ Gas filter
- ✔ Oil filter
- ✔ Transmission filter

Lisa's Tip

Have the replacement date or mileage marked on the gas, air and oil filters in black marker. It will never rub off!

The Tune-Up

There is a kind of harmony to a well-tuned car when all the parts are working in concert with one another, so the concept of a tune-up strikes a chord with car owners and mechanics alike. I'm sorry to tell you we don't really use the term "tune-up" anymore. In fact, it's no accident that I've used so many physiological analogies, because these days you really do bring your car in for a seasonal checkup.

Most cars today are more technologically sound and have longer-lasting parts than their predecessors. There was a time when, once a year, you would bring your car to the garage to change the plugs, cap the rotor and wires, change the oil, change the air filter, slap down $100 and not worry about it until next year, so long as nothing went wrong in the interim. These days, different things need to be checked at different times. Some parts and components can last up to 25,000 to 35,000 miles (40,000 to 60,000 km) before you need to have them checked.

However, spark plugs should still be looked at once a year. An oil change is usually standard, but not all of what were once considered tune-up parts, such as belts, hoses and the lighting system, need to be changed each time. Some garages offer seasonal packages, specials that include an oil change, a scan test and a 15-point inspection. It's not a bad idea to take advantage of these deals. As long as it's within the maintenance schedule recommended by your dealer, and thus within your warranty (meaning that any needed repairs would be covered), it can't hurt to take your car in for a checkup if you think it'll save you a couple bucks.

They say the cynic knows the cost of everything and the value of nothing. If you are a cynic, you might believe a seasonal checkup simply gets you into the garage more often, putting more money into your mechanic's pocket. And you'd be right. But it only makes sense to make sure your car is in good working order for the winter, doesn't it? And when the spring thaw hits, you probably should see that your suspension is up to scratch. Rule of thumb: follow your car's maintenance schedule, but know enough about your car so that you're getting the service you need without paying for stuff you don't.

You are now well on your way to impressing your mechanic friends at their crazy automotive parties. Not only can you toss around the terms, but also probably have some idea of what you're talking about. Keep in mind everything we talked about in this chapter, and I suspect you will start to care more about your car. It will appreciate it, believe me. But don't let your newfound confidence translate into overconfidence behind the wheel. There are still some things you need to know about driver safety. Keep reading.

3

For Safety's Sake

When you get behind the wheel you are indeed taking your life into your own hands. Remember that your car is basically a 2,000 pound (900 kg) explosive device. Your driving habits, as well as how well you take care of your car, affect others on the road—which is why you're always being told not to drink and drive. We also know about the dangers of talking on a cell phone while driving; experts say that even hands-free units are a dangerous distraction. Experts also say that eating and drinking at the wheel puts you at risk, with the most dangerous beverage being hot coffee. Makes you think twice, doesn't it?

Proper car maintenance is no less important to your safety than sober and alert driving. In the last chapter we talked about the things you need to do to keep your car on the road. But there are a few other things that directly affect your safety, as well as that of your passengers and fellow drivers, so I've devoted this chapter to the maintenance of your tires, brakes, suspension and steering. If anything goes wrong with any one of these, you may no longer be in control of the car. Clint Eastwood as Dirty Harry might say, "You gotta ask yourself one question: Do I feel lucky?" With a one-ton explosive device in your hands, at high speed, with no control...Do you feel lucky?

Tires

Your tires are your connection to the road, and as such they demand proper care and maintenance. Think of your tires as the soles of your car's shoes—or maybe even as your car's fingerprints. Anthropologists say that fingerprints helped early humanoids to grip and climb without slipping. That's exactly what your tires are for; to keep your car on the road. Let's take a closer look.

Tire Cross-Section

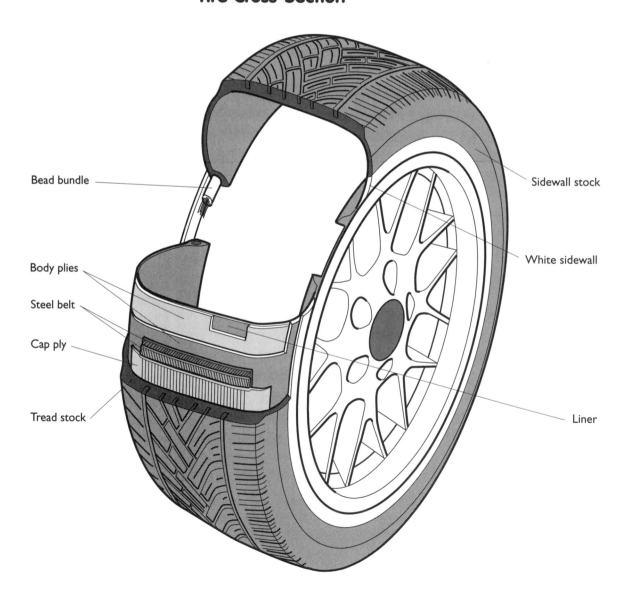

Bead bundle

Body plies

Steel belt

Cap ply

Tread stock

Sidewall stock

White sidewall

Liner

Tire construction

Most of us conventionally think of the tire as separate from the wheel, or the rim. The rim is the part of the wheel that's covered by a hubcap. The tire fits onto the rim, and is much more than a simple thick rubber skin.

Tire carcass

Tire carcass is a bit of a nasty term that sounds like you're describing something dead at the side of the road—rubber roadkill, as it were. That's somewhat disconcerting when you think of all the blown and shredded tires you've seen along the side of a highway. But the carcass is basically the skeleton of the tire, the bones that help the tire to keep its shape. It can be made up of a combination of rubber, nylon, polyester and other materials.

Belts

Most conventional tires are **steel-belted radials**. Thin steel belts make up the part of the tire carcass that runs just underneath the tread, like a layer of muscle beneath the skin. This kind of tire is called a "radial" because the belts run along the radius of the tire, from bead (where the tire meets the rim) to bead, providing extra support to the tread itself.

A Tire by Any Other Name...

Back in the '50s, driving a car was an adventure. There was no such thing as steel-belted radials in those days. Tires were skinny, and made out of materials ranging from fiberglass and nylon to polyester! In the late '60s and early '70s, radials were introduced, and driving became a much more reliable mode of transportation!

Tread

Your tire's outer layer—the part that you see—is the tread. It's like the skin that covers the carcass. And, like your epidermis, it has another layer of skin just underneath. In the tire's case, this second layer is called the undertread.

Like the sole of a shoe, a tire's tread is where most of the wear and tear happens. When you're driving, only about a palm-sized surface of the tire is ever in contact with the road. With so much pressure riding on so little, it's very important to pay proper attention to the upkeep of your tires.

The writing on the wall

There are different kinds of treads for different tires. Some treads have very specific purposes, like displacing water or pushing away snow. There are different sizes of tires for different kinds of cars, and even for different types of driving. The "sidewall" is the part of the tire between the tread and the bead. That's where you'll find all the information about the tire itself: its type, weight capacity and maximum air pressure. You probably already know a little bit about tire pressure, and you might even have your own tire gauge somewhere in your glove box. It's one of those basic tools that drivers keep on hand; checking the tire pressure and the oil when we fill up makes us feel like we know something about cars.

One of the pieces of information you'll find on the sidewall is the tire's maximum air pressure. Air pressure is measured in "psi," or "pounds per square inch." Most conventional tires will take up to 35 psi. Some larger cars, SUVs and trucks may need more to support their heavier weight. You'll notice that the bottom edges of your tires bulge out a bit on either side of the tire tread. That's the air being displaced by the weight of the car and all the stuff and people in it.

Get out your decoder ring

The other information on the wall of your tire is in code. Not a secret code, mind you, so you won't need an Enigma machine to understand it. It's a simple series of letters and numbers that tell you all you need to know about your tire. For instance, your tire might say something like "P195/75 R14." The P stands for "passenger," which indicates the kind of vehicle you drive, and thus the type of tire your car requires. In other words, the tires on your car are passenger tires. The rest of the information refers to the measurements of various parts of the tire surface when the tire is filled to proper inflation capacity. So, with 35 psi of air packed into your tire, the contact surface of the tread—the part of the tire that is actually on the road—should measure 195 mm (7.7 inches) in width. Then comes what we call the "aspect ratio," which is basically a percentage. On a tire that reads "P195/75 R14," the number 75 means that the height of that portion of the sidewall that runs from the contact surface (the road) up to the bead (where it attaches to the rim) works out to 75 percent of the width of the contact surface itself. Sounds complicated, I know, but this information helps to determine your car's weight capacity, which is also written on the sidewall. Again, all this information assumes that the tire is filled to proper capacity. The R means "radial." In our example, the 14 refers to the size of the rim or wheel itself, which in this case would indicate 14 inches.

> **Lisa's Tip**
> Once a month, inspect your tires for uneven tread wear, cuts or cracks, bulges, foreign objects or any other sign of trouble.

You will also find information about the "speed rating" of your tires, represented by the letter S or T. That tells you that the tire should be good, under normal pressure, up to speeds of 110 to 120 mph (180 to 190 km/h). You know, like if you're on the autobahn. Where we live, though, that's just way too fast.

Can't take the pressure?

Heat expands and cold contracts. Your tire pressure will increase in the summer heat and decrease in the winter cold. Some people will put a bit more air in their tires during the winter to compensate. Conversely, there are some drivers who let a little air out of their tires in the summer. But the best thing to do is to check the tires regularly and keep them at the manufacturer's recommended pressure level.

There are no small parts

Don't ignore your **tire valve**—that little doodad sticking out of the rim where the air goes in. Bicycle tires have them, too, and both cyclists and drivers have been known to lose the little black rubber cap that fits over the top. Most people think it doesn't matter, that no air will escape if the cap is not on. Technically this is correct, but that little cap is important, and its loss could lead to a leak. The tire valve cap keeps dirt and moisture from getting into the valve, both of which can cause some damage and could eventually lead to air seepage. Your tire may not deflate without the little black cap, but you do need it. Watch where it goes; don't let it roll away from you when you're filling your tires with air. If you've actually lost yours, you can buy another through the dealership, or through an aftermarket parts dealer.

Winter tires

Remember that the treads of your tires are the soles of your car's shoes, and basically serve the same purpose. Just as you have different types of footwear to suit different kinds of weather, so you need to change your tires when and where the climate warrants. If you live in snowy climes, then you need winter tires. You wouldn't wear sandals in the winter, would you? Then why would you drive on summer tires in snowy conditions? If you're plowing through snow and sleet on summer tires, you're putting yourself and others in danger. All-season tires just won't cut it, by the way—they just don't handle as well under bad conditions. You need proper snow tires for the winter months.

Why Four?

These days, transportation regulators stress the necessity of changing all four tires for the winter season. Why? It's a matter of safety. With four tires specially equipped for performance on ice and snow, your car brakes better, steers better and handles better. If you drive an SUV and think the rules don't apply to you, think again. In this case, being bigger isn't necessarily better. Because your vehicle is both taller and heavier than a car, stopping becomes even more of an issue.

Brakes

I introduced you briefly to your brake system in Chapter 1, and you got an idea of how brake fluid works in Chapter 2. I can't stress enough how important it is to take good care of your braking system. It's a fairly involved system, extending from the pedal all the way up to the brake warning light on the

The Braking System

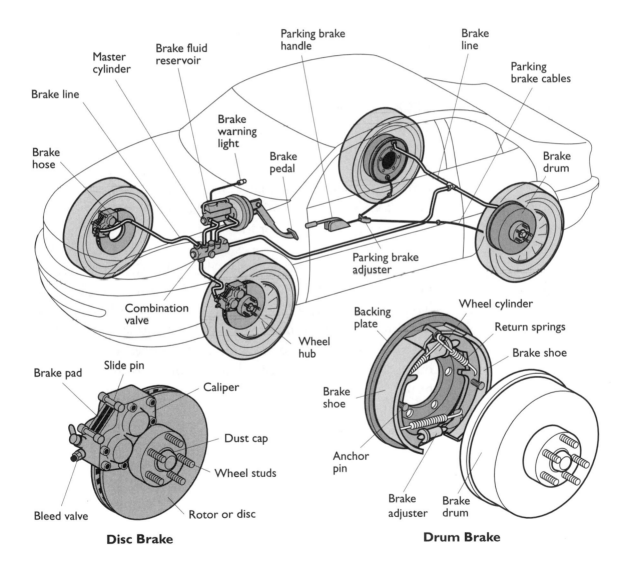

Disc Brake

Drum Brake

dashboard and including all the parts in between. It includes things like a vacuum power booster, a brake fluid reservoir and master cylinder (where the fluid is stored), the steel brake lines that carry fluid to the brake components along the flexible hoses, and something called a combination valve. And then, of course, there's the parking brake, with its handle, adjuster and cables. And we haven't even touched the wheels yet, where all the slowing and stopping takes place.

Mechanics refer to break shoes and pads as the brake friction material because they use friction to slow and stop your car. Your braking system consists of **brake drums** and **shoes** in the rear, which work when the shoes expand against the inside of the drums, and **brake calipers** and **pads** in the front that squeeze what's called the **brake rotor**, kind of like the brakes on a bicycle.

Brake problems

There are several different problems that can affect the braking system. Customers generally complain about these problems in similar ways—and mechanics become familiar with these complaints. You might say that your car doesn't stop well—or doesn't stop at all. You might find that you're pressing harder on the pedal than usual, or that it's taking longer than normal to stop, or that the pedal goes all the way to the floor. All of these symptoms could mean that the brake friction material is out of adjustment or worn out. Or the disc/drum surface may have been worn down or roughed up (it should have a glass-smooth surface). It may need to be resurfaced, buffed or replaced. Possibly the brake linings (the shoes and pads) are burned, which might mean that you drove with your hand-brake slightly engaged; the heat caused by the constant application of the brakes can cause the brake linings to crack and the drums to overheat and warp, resulting in brake failure.

Some customers complain that their car pulls to one side when they brake. That could indicate a tire problem. (If the tires are not inflated properly, the car will pull when you step on the brake.) Or you could have a defective **wheel cylinder** or brake caliper, which means that your brake friction material is not being applied correctly or that you have a fluid leak somewhere. You might describe your brakes as too sensitive. That could mean that the brake linings are soaked with brake fluid or that the brake friction material is out of adjustment.

And let's not forget about all the noise your brakes could make. Squeaky or noisy brakes could indicate one of several things. Your brake linings might be worn out, or you might have incorrect new friction material—which means that although you've recently had new brakes put on your car, your mechanic used a brand of brake friction material that isn't quite compatible with your vehicle. When I'm changing a customer's brakes, I normally use simple store-bought brake friction material. But sometimes I have to use the same material the original manufacturer used because the new ones aren't compatible with a particular car model.

Brake squeal could also be caused by rust buildup between the components. That's right: moisture + metal = rust. When you have the brakes serviced, ask your mechanic to remove all the rust from the system's contact points.

Noisy sounds and awkward responses are a brake system's desperate cries for help. You must be tuned in to your car. When I worked as a mechanic at a major chain, I was shocked by a customer who came in complaining that his brakes felt "funny," and that there was a noise, a noise he claimed had only just started. When I took a peek behind the wheel, I was aghast. His front disc brakes had been worn down to the point where there was hardly any disc left. I'd never seen anything like it. He'd managed to chew straight through the disc brake rotor, something I'd thought was impossible. Despite what he had told me, he'd been driving on badly worn brakes for a long time. The parts were so badly worn that we kept them at the garage to show our clients the lunacy that exists behind the steering wheel of some cars today.

So remember: if you hear a noise, or if something just doesn't feel right, get your brakes checked.

Signs and symptoms

Here's a quick look at some of the most common symptoms of a braking system gone wrong. Ignore at your own peril! The longer a problem exists, the more it will probably cost you to fix.

Symptom	What it might mean
It's taking longer to stop	Brakes worn down
You feel a pulsing in your brakes or steering	Brake rotors overmachined or warped
Your car pulls to one side when stopping	Caliper problem; bad wheel cylinder; alignment is off
Your car vibrates when stopping	Calipers seized or rotors that are out of round
Your car makes a grinding noise when stopping	Brakes worn out
Your brakes squeal or shriek	Brakes worn out

The dual brake system

Most cars today are equipped with a **dual brake system**. Older cars used a single-piston master cylinder brake system. All the brake lines were hooked up to one circuit, which meant that a fluid leak in one wheel would affect all of the others. If there was ever a problem, you'd lose braking power in all four wheels. Needless to say, this proved very dangerous.

A dual system uses two mechanisms, one that operates the front brakes and another that operates the rear. The advantage is that if there is a leak you don't lose all braking ability. Some smaller cars use a diagonally split system, which means that a front wheel and a rear wheel will be on the same channel. But the principle is the same. If there is a leak, you'll still have two wheels that stop the car. But that doesn't mean the leak should go unattended. Have it fixed immediately, because when you're driving a one-ton hunk of metal, two brakes ain't gonna cut it.

Antilock brake system (ABS)

We all have a tendency to jam on the brakes when we need to stop in a hurry. And "jam" is a good word, because that's exactly what used to happen to brakes: they'd jam or lock, leaving you in a real jam if, say, the car skidded or slid on ice. The antilock brake system (ABS) solved that problem—to an extent. Your car's ABS uses a computer to control the pressure on the brakes by pumping them automatically. When you hit the brakes suddenly, you'll feel a pulse. That's the ABS kicking in. It prevents the wheels from locking so that you won't skid. Those of you used to driving in winter conditions might recall a time when you'd have to physically pump your brakes to avoid sliding on black ice. Nowadays, the ABS does that for you. A computer can detect when your wheels are sliding on a slippery surface and when you're putting sudden pressure on the brakes. As if the sudden pressure of your panicked foot were a cry for help, the computer responds by pumping the brakes to slow you down. But a word of caution: many drivers get overconfident when they've got ABS in their cars. You still need a proper braking distance; just because you've got ABS brakes doesn't mean you can get closer to the driver in front of you. And if you're the kind of driver who likes to come up right behind the slowpokes to force them over, bear in mind that regardless of how good your brakes are, if the driver in front of you suddenly brakes, you're in trouble.

Lisa's Tip
If the ABS light on the dashboard comes on, there's a reason. Don't take it for granted. Have it checked.

ABS brakes are not problem-free. The most common complaint we get involves "wheel-speed sensor failure." The ABS indicator light could go on, indicating that the computer has noticed a fault in the ABS. This could mean one of several things. The computer might not be "reading" or "receiving" a speed signal from one or more of the car's wheels, or it might be trying to apply the ABS, but something in the hydraulic unit is all gummed up. If that's the case, it usually means an expensive trip to the garage.

After having their brakes serviced, some customers come back after a short time to say that the ABS light is still on, which probably means that the sensor is not working properly or that a reluctor ring is cracked. A **reluctor ring** is basically a gear. If it's cracked, or if one of the cogs is broken, it will mislead the computer into thinking that a wheel is spinning at the wrong speed. The computer misinterprets this information and mistakenly applies the ABS.

The components of an ABS are so fragile that even a seasoned mechanic might break them by mistake and not be aware of it. Sometimes all it takes is a slight tap on a sensor to cause it to crack. Add a little water or humidity, and a couple of days later the ABS light comes on. Thankfully, with new advances in technology, these problems are becoming rare. Sensors are stronger, they're placed in safer areas and they're protected from the elements and from mechanics' clumsy hands.

In the Right Direction: Your Steering System

In Chapter 1 we talked a bit about the rack-and-pinion steering system. This is a hydraulic system, which means that it uses a fluid to set mechanical parts in motion. The steering wheel is quite literally your hands-on connection to the wheels of your car. You are in control—until something goes wrong.

There are actually two types of steering on today's cars: conventional rack-and-pinion steering and a **parallelogram steering system**. The parallelogram system is found in most large rear-wheel-drive cars and light-duty trucks. This is the system that takes the most grease. Most cars use the rack-and-pinion type, though, so we'll focus on that.

Most complaints about steering involve a noise (usually a kind of a whine), difficulty steering, or a tendency for the car to pull to one side while braking. These problems could be caused by badly adjusted brakes, uneven tire pressure, bad wheel alignment or loose front-end components. (You see, auto mechanics is like holistic medicine: in the end you need to treat the whole car, since many of its parts affect one another.)

She Rides Like a Dream: The Suspension

The suspension is not just about a comfortable ride. It is the entire support system of your car. No suspension, no support. You can't sleep too well on a cheap mattress and box spring; if your bed is too soft, you'll bounce around more than necessary and wake up with a bad back or a stiff neck. Your car also needs proper support.

Most cars today use the **MacPherson strut suspension**. It's named for Earl S. MacPherson, who at one time was Ford's chief engineer. There is also the **double-wishbone suspension**. Although it's older, some cars, such as the Mazda Miata, still use it because of its precision. It's called "wishbone" because of the shape of one of its components. Both systems, with their springs, coils and shock absorbers, allow the car's body and **chassis** (the underbody) to move up and down while absorbing the shock of the bumps in the road. The suspension has several other components, such as **control arms**, which link the wheels to the frame or body, and **stabilizer bars**, which prevent the car from leaning while cornering, thus improving stability at high speeds. And there are assorted other springs, links and bushings (small plastic cushions) that make for a smooth ride. But with all the bouncing around your car does on different types of roads, and with all of its weight, several things can go wrong.

Loose front-end components—like **tie-rod ends** (little ball-and-socket joints that help the wheels pivot and turn)—could lead to a loose feeling in the steering wheel. If you find that there's too much play in the wheel, meaning that you're able to turn your steering wheel too far in either direction without the wheels reacting, this could be the cause. Loose parts mean more room to move around, hence the loose feel in the steering.

If your steering wheel springs back to central position too quickly when you turn the car, you could have a problem with the MacPherson strut suspension, specifically a problem with the bearing plate (the part that allows the strut to pivot). You'll probably also hear a creaking sound, and should have your suspension inspected. (We'll get into the different sounds your car makes, and what they mean, in the next chapter.)

If you're finding it hard to steer, and if you've ruled out a problem with the power steering and the alignment, then you may have a stiff ball joint. A **ball joint** is a pivot point for the wheel mounting. If it is indeed stiff, it needs lubrication, or it needs to be replaced.

These things are important, as I stressed in the beginning of the chapter, because your life, the lives of your passengers and the lives of the other drivers on the road and pedestrians are at stake.

Here's an example of why you shouldn't take any of this for granted. The Honda Civic has what's called an upper ball joint, which is part of the upper wishbone and allows the wheel to pivot. A customer came in with his Honda Civic on a tow truck. The wheel was tilted at an unnatural angle and the axle was broken. He would have had some looseness to his steering and would probably have heard a noise, like a knocking sound, when he went over bumps. All he had to do was to take the car into the shop to have a simple ball joint replaced and the wheels aligned. But he ignored his car's cries for help, endangering himself and others. While he was driving, part of the front-end suspension came loose, as did one of the wheels. In fact, the wheel actually bent over. Try to imagine what that looks like! He lost control of his car and miraculously avoided hitting anyone. But instead of only having a ball joint replacement and a wheel alignment, he now needed a new ball joint, a new tire and a new axle shaft, since his got yanked out of the transmission. With the added cost of the towing, he ended up paying close to $900 and had to deal with the inconvenience of being without his car for two days. And he's lucky to be alive.

4

Diagnosing Your Car's Symptoms

Imagine yourself as a world-renowned physician, perhaps the best diagnostician in the country, knowing exactly what's wrong with your patient just by hearing him cough. Learning to diagnose car trouble on your own is a lot like that.

A good car owner develops a relationship with his car over time. You come to depend on one another; you depend on your car for transportation, and your car depends on you for care. As in any relationship, it's important that you become a good listener. Not that you and your car will ever sit down for a heart-to-heart, but eventually, as your car gets on in years and little things begin to fall apart, you'll start to hear sounds, little noises that weren't there before. Your car might also begin to "feel" different, with a pull to the left here, a loose steering wheel there. Think of these sounds and sensations as your car's cries for help; it really is trying to tell you something. In this chapter I'm going to teach you to speak its language. In the next chapter we'll talk about how to find the right garage and the right mechanic. Wouldn't it be satisfying if, after checking out your own car and taking it to the garage, the mechanic came back to you and said, "You were right"? That could well happen after I've helped you develop an ear for car trouble and for car talk. By the end of this chapter you'll have the necessary tools to engage in meaningful dialogue with your mechanic.

And for My Next Impression...: Explaining Your Car's Problems

I get the same thing from people who call in to my radio show as I do from customers who come into the garage: "My car makes a funny noise," they tell me. I ask, "What kind of noise?" and things fall apart from there. "I don't know," they say, smiling sheepishly, "a funny noise." Well, as a mechanic, I need you to make that noise. Specific problems come with specific sounds. The more information you provide, the better I'll be able to help you. Like many people, you may have a hard time making silly noises. You may be shy or embarrassed, and you may be afraid we'll laugh at you. Well, rest assured: we will laugh at you. But only after you've left the shop.

Your imitations of your car's noises are the starting point of an important dialogue between you and your mechanic, someone you should be able to trust as much as you trust your doctor, or the person who cuts your hair. You wouldn't want your stylist to get your bangs wrong. Similarly, if your car has bangs, you'll want to be as specific as you can about where and when you heard them, and if it was in fact a "bang" you heard and not a "knock."

When you come into the shop with a noise, your mechanic should be asking you the right questions based on the noises you say your car is making, and not just getting you to make silly noises for the sake of making silly noises. As I said, there are some very specific sounds associated with specific problems, and as mechanics we know them all. You might say your car goes "bang bang bang." But it might actually be something more along the lines of a "knock knock knock," or even a "toc toc toc." And if you can't talk the toc, then we can't walk the walk. If you tell me your car is knocking, I might say, "Are you sure it's not more like a banging?" The two of us are suddenly engaged in this ritual song and dance, both of us making funny noises at one another as we try to zero in on your car's problem and how best to fix it.

Speaking car

What the heck is a tic, and how is it different from a toc? Help is at hand!

The Sound Your Car Is Making	A Real-Life Equivalent
chirp	a bird
creak	an old door with rusty hinges
knock	your knuckles on a wooden door
squeal	a car turning a corner too quickly
tic	an old-fashioned stop watch
toc	A hollow tapping sound (like a pen against a water bottle)

Your mechanic should be able to help you to fine-tune the noise by asking you other questions: When does the car make the noise? Does it happen in the rain? Do you hear it on the highway? Or when you're going uphill? Does a dashboard light come on? Tell your mechanic as much as you can, and don't withhold any information. The more she knows, the better. You want to avoid unnecessary exploratory surgery for your car; if your mechanic has to go in there and look around for a problem, you're talkin' extra labor charges. A simple rattle, if properly diagnosed, could indicate something as basic as a loose clamp on your exhaust system, which should cost you only a few dollars. In some cases, your mechanic might charge you only for the price of the clamp itself, and not the labor, but only if the two of you can get to the root of the problem through this game of charades.

My goal is to get you to recognize on your own what needs fixing so you can go to your mechanic and tell her what's wrong, rather than simply tossing her the keys and saying, "Fix my car." That's like handing your mechanic a blank check, and some unscrupulous grease monkeys will gladly take advantage of that situation.

You may have a problem as small as a burned-out lightbulb. For example, if your turn signal doesn't work properly and the little dashboard light just stays on, that's telling you that one of the lightbulbs in either the front or rear signals needs to be changed. That's easy to assess: just get out of the car and have a look at which light is burned out. You can either have your mechanic change it for you, or you can change it yourself and save a couple of bucks. Many of the problems we'll talk about in this chapter can be do-it-yourself jobs. I'll teach you how to tinker under the hood—and even how to change that simple lightbulb—in the do-it-yourself guide in Chapter 6. For now, let's get into some diagnostics.

Rude Noises

It's great if your car is turning heads, but not if it's for the wrong reasons. If folks are turning around wondering "who did it," and you're crouching behind the dash, embarrassed because your car's making rude noises, you've probably got a hole in your bottom. That is to say you've developed a hole, either

The Exhaust System

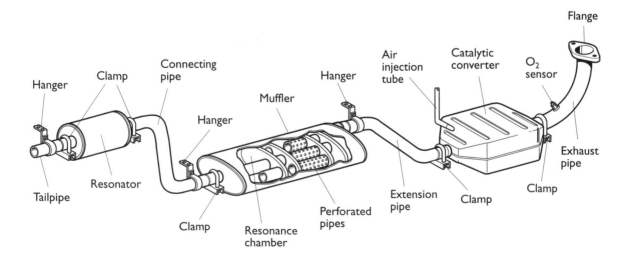

from corrosion or from a puncture, in the part of the **exhaust system** that runs along the bottom of your car. The exhaust system extends from the engine manifold, down along the belly of the car, all the way to the **tailpipe**. Somewhere along the line is your **catalytic converter** (your car's environmental/waste management system) and the **muffler**, so called because it muffles the loud and throaty rumbling a car engine makes. But if there is a problem—a hole or a crack of some kind—then your car will be blowin' raspberries all over town.

Leaks can occur anywhere along the exhaust system. Some leaks are relatively quiet, others can be quite loud. If the hole is closer to the engine, that is to say, farther away from the muffler, the rumble will be louder. A leak can also be accompanied by the smell of exhaust in the car. That's a little tricky. Exhaust is basically carbon monoxide, which is an odorless gas. If you do smell it, it means your engine is not running well, and something, most probably unburned gasoline, has leaked into the exhaust system. In other words, the carbon monoxide is "contaminated." You'll probably hear the noise before you actually smell anything. In any case, there's probably a hole somewhere along the line, which more often than not is caused by rust. A word of caution: Exhaust leaks can be deadly. If you think you might have a problem, get it checked out immediately.

Have you ever seen water dripping from a tailpipe, either yours or someone else's? That's a good thing, as Martha Stewart might say. You want your exhaust system to drain off any excess water from the exhaust system. Remember: water + metal = rust! But when the car is stopped, any water that might have been in the process of being drained off stays trapped inside the pipe, which can lead to rust and corrosion. The regular movement of the pipe—there is always some natural play—will eventually cause some kind of breakage, a hole or a crack, and thus the throaty rumble. That means a trip to the garage to have the exhaust system repaired.

Rattle and hum in the catalytic converter

The exhaust that comes out of your tailpipe is "clean exhaust" because it's been filtered through the catalytic converter, part of your car's antipollution system. I'll explain later how this converter works and why you need it. It's a fairly sophisticated, high-tech device that shouldn't break or make any noise, unless you've hit something, or your engine is not running correctly. When that happens, it usually rattles.

Some customers come into a garage and tell the mechanic that their catalytic converter has worn down, a complaint that usually raises some eyebrows. The catalytic converter shouldn't wear down in a car that's less than 10 years old, unless someone has dumped unnecessary additives into the gas tank or the oil. If that's the case, then the engine may run incorrectly, either too hot or too cold. If it runs too hot, the catalytic converter could melt on the inside. If the engine runs too cold, the catalytic converter can't do its job, so gas fumes get in and contaminate it.

Too often, drivers have their converters changed because of a misdiagnosis. If you tell me you've had your catalytic converter changed but you can't tell me the specific reason why, such as a spark plug misfire, then chances are good that you'll have to change it again in six months to a year. You may have had an immediate symptom fixed, but the underlying problem that caused the malfunction is still there. The only time a mechanic should even think about changing your catalytic converter is when you tell him either that you drove over something and then heard a rattle, or that you bought the car secondhand and it came with a rattling catalytic converter.

Shake, rattle and roll: Diagnosing the source

Of course, an aging car makes all kinds of noises, rattles and rumbles, so how are you supposed to know if a noise comes from the catalytic converter or the exhaust system? Give it a shake. Make sure the car is turned off, and give it time to cool down. Then get down on your hands and knees, grab the tailpipe and give it a shake. Take a little rubber hammer and tap around the exhaust system. Listen for the rattle. Some catalytic converters have porcelain inside them, while others contain what's called a "glass pack." If either is broken you should hear a ringing sound, almost like two coffee cups clinking together. See if anything moves around. If you can get under the car, or jack it up (see Chapter 3 for some safety concerns), look for the telltale signs of black soot in certain areas. That should tell you if it's your catalytic converter or an exhaust leak: exhaust leaks leave a soot stain at the site of the leak. You might also hear the sound while driving, particularly when you accelerate. Make a note of that so you can discuss it with your mechanic.

Remember that the catalytic converter is part of the exhaust system. If you ignore its cries for help, if it's broken and goes unchecked for too long, it could jam up the system, trapping exhaust inside. That will affect your car's performance. Trapped exhaust basically chokes the system, obstructing the flow of exhaust. If you allow that problem to fester, the exhaust system could burn up, even turn red like the element on your stovetop, and your car could catch fire. That's where the heat shields come in.

Heat shields entered the vernacular with the advent of NASA's space shuttle program. Shuttle launches have been delayed in the past, or even canceled altogether, because of defective heat shields. In the tragic case of the shuttle *Columbia* in February 2003, the heat shields actually tore off on re-entry, leading to severe overheating, fire and explosion. The crew never had a chance.

Just like on the space shuttle's underbelly, there are heat shields bolted to sections of the underside of your car, protecting it from heat generated by the exhaust system. Loose heat shields will make a more tinny-sounding rattle. Say you're about to leave your driveway. You've just taken your foot off the brake, but just before you step on the gas pedal you hear a noise, almost like someone tapping on sheet metal. That's the sound of loose heat shields. Don't ignore that sound; it just might save your car from the ravages of fire. A NASA report published in August 2003 said that similar problems that persist within the shuttle program go unchecked for too long, and that lax safety procedures likely led to the deaths of the crew. Think of your car as your own little shuttle, and your family as the crew. Now you'll begin to understand the importance of proper car maintenance: a badly maintained car is unsafe.

Good, and Bad, Vibrations

Remember that there are some noises, sounds and vibrations that are considered normal. If you're not used to ABS brakes, for example, you might get a little freaked out when they engage and the brake pedal vibrates back against your foot. That's just the normal pulsation that prevents your wheels from locking in a dangerous, slippery situation. On the other hand—or the other foot, as the case may be—there are instances of brake vibration or pedal pulsation that should serve as a warning. For example, suppose you step on the brakes and the car vibrates, the dashboard rattles, the steering column and steering wheel shake, and maybe even the whole body of the car shakes and rattles. That could mean that your brake caliper has partially seized, leaving the brakes partially engaged. This will cause your discs to overheat and probably warp, and your brakes will feel "lumpy" when you push on the pedal. You can also get rust buildup in the brake system if the caliper is not working properly. The rust makes for uneven surfaces that rub together, causing a vibration. This can be fixed by machining the disc surface or replacing the disc itself. Unclean, rusted surfaces and overheated and warped rotors and drums need attention. Heed their cries for help.

Car convulsions

Some car owners complain of high-speed shaking. You can feel it in the steering wheel and in your feet, legs, hands and arms. This could indicate a tire problem. Most tire problems become evident only above 40 to 50 mph (65 to 80 km/h). But you can sometimes feel tire vibrations at speeds as low as 20 mph (30 km/h). Usually these vibrations indicate unevenly worn tires or wheels that are not properly balanced.

If your car is shaking at high speeds, and you think you might have tire trouble, the first thing to do is to pull over and check the tires. Look for bumps, bulges, cuts and other deformities. Or you might have lost the wheel weight. A tire is never perfect in its construction, and it might therefore be a bit heavier or lighter on one side. At high speeds, the uneven weight causes the wheel to vibrate, making it feel as if you're driving over train tracks. To balance out the tire, car manufacturers will often hang a small weight, attached to the rim on the opposite side of the so-called high spot (where the uneven weight is). Sometimes the weight falls off. If that's the case, you might find a clean spot on the tire where the wheel weight once was.

If you're driving in winter conditions, a buildup of snow and ice, or dirt, could make for an unbalanced tire. If these things don't seem to be the cause of the problem, the next thing to do is to have a look at the underside of the car. There could be some damage to the front end that you might miss when you're giving your car the once-over at the side of the road. So take it in to your mechanic and have him put the car up on a lift to check things out. You could also have a problem with the wheel itself. Maybe you've damaged it by hitting a pothole (or one of your kids did and didn't tell you). If the wheel is no longer "round" you'll have vibrations or noise when driving.

We've talked about all the knocks, tics and tocs your car can make. Well, tires can also knock. Tire knocking—which actually makes a "toc toc toc" sound—could indicate that your sidewalls are not stiff enough for your car's particular application. That means, quite simply, that you've got the wrong tires on your car. They may be perfectly good tires, just not the right ones. For example, they might not be the correct speed rating for your vehicle; some cars are heavier and require a higher speed rating to give you better stability on the highway.

Driving around in a haunted house: Your car's creaky sounds

You're waiting to do a three-point turn into a driveway or a parking spot. You signal, take your foot off the brake and turn your wheel...and you're spooked because you hear a creaking, just like an old cobweb-covered door in a haunted house. That's not necessarily a reflection of the state of your car, and don't be scared, there are no monsters in the back seat. That could be your ball joint talking, a thirsty ball joint, croaking for lack of lubrication. You probably need what we call a lube job, where a mechanic will inject grease into all the little grease fittings to lubricate the components. With newer cars, however, manufacturers are making ball joints that don't require lubrication. If you're driving a newer model and you still hear this sound, have your car looked at. You might need to have the ball joint replaced.

A worn bushing can also creak. A **bushing** is a rubber or plastic washer-like piece that provides cushioning between two moving parts. You can find some on parts of your suspension system, as well as in other areas of your car. They can wear out either from age or from grease or oil contamination. If that's the case, you'll hear a creaking similar to that caused by a ball joint, but shorter in duration. Again, you'll want to be sure of exactly what kind of sound you hear and when you're hearing it. Are you driving or turning? Answers to questions like that will help you and your mechanic determine if it's a ball joint or a bushing.

The jerk behind the wheel

Do you feel a jerk behind the wheel? You're being too hard on yourself! Seriously, though, if a creaking sound is accompanied by a jerk at the wheel, especially if you're stopped, it could be that the bearing for the shock absorber in the front end has worn down and is seizing up. Your steering wheel might also feel tight, then loose, then tight again. It's a rare problem, but one you need to have looked at.

I hear you knockin'...

Differentiating between all of these noises is like learning music. You need to develop an ear to tell the difference between a toc and a knock. We've already talked the tocs, now let's talk about knocks—and thunks, clacks and ticks.

Indeed, a knock can mean many things. If you hear a knock when you're turning either left or right in a car with front-wheel drive, you could have a bad constant velocity joint, or **CV joint**, as we call it. That's the axle that transfers torque to the wheels, the power that actually makes them spin. There are a few large ball bearings held in place by a kind of a cage. If you hear it going knock knock knock, or even toc toc toc, it may mean that the axle itself needs to be replaced. This is important. If you don't have this looked at, you could end up losing

Lisa's Tip

If you think you might have a squeaky bushing and you want to check it yourself, simply spray a little water on the suspected bushing. If the noise goes away for a short time, you've found the right one. This way you can save yourself some money on the time and labor it would've taken your mechanic to find it.

control of your car or in need of a major repair (remember the guy with the Honda Civic?). There are some sounds that you can also *feel*, like a thunk, for example. When you put the car in gear, either in drive or in reverse, you might hear the car go thunk. Even if you have your foot on the brake (which you should while putting it in gear), you might still feel the car "thunk" forward or backward, almost as if it's just a little too eager to get going. In the worst-case scenario, it could be a problem with the transmission. More than likely, though, it's a problem with what we call engine support or transmission support, meaning the cushions between the power train and the chassis.

Moving on up into the engine, you want to keep an ear cocked for clacking. Think about the sound of the front door of your old school closing slowly behind you when the steel latch "clacked" into place, or maybe even the sound of a jail-cell door (funny how those two always sounded the same to me). The clacks will either be fast or slow, depending on your speed, and might be accompanied by a light on the dash indicating low oil pressure. If this happens, stop the car immediately and check your oil. You might have a defective **valve lifter** or some sort of engine problem. But mechanics tend to associate the sound with low oil pressure. And as I mentioned in a previous chapter, driving on low oil pressure could scrap the engine. "But Lisa," you say, "what if I'm in the middle of nowhere, with no cell phone, no oil and no mechanic in sight?" Pull over and start walkin', or stay put and wait for help. Seriously. We don't know how long you've been driving like that, and we don't know how much farther you could have gone without putting yourself and others in serious danger. This way you'll eventually find help, and you'll still have a car to go back to.

Don't be alarmed if your engine is ticking. I know I described the internal combustion engine as an explosive device, but if you hear ticking it doesn't mean your engine has suddenly become a time bomb. Maybe if you're Tony Soprano. But *you* don't have to worry about this kind of thing, right? Some customers have described the sound as more of a clicking, or even a soft clacking, and it usually means that the valve lash adjustment is off. That means that there is too big a clearance between the top of the valve and its connection components. You're actually hearing the valve opening and closing. Again, don't be alarmed, but do go have it checked, because when an adjustment like this is off parts can age prematurely, causing your engine to run badly.

Some car owners complain about ticking sounds either in a new car or in a newly bought pre-owned car, and usually on start-up. They're actually hearing more of a click. That's the sound of the **fuel injectors** working. It's one of those normal sounds that you just have to get used to.

A squeal or a screech indicates a problem with **fan belts** that's been virtually eliminated in newer cars. You probably hear it when you accelerate, and it indicates a belt that needs servicing, probably because it's slipping. If you want to find the source of the squeal, toss a few drops of water on a moving belt. The noise should go away for a few seconds. If it comes back soon after, you'll know which belt needs servicing. In newer cars, however, belts have been manufactured with self-adjusting belt tensioners, which help prevent slippage; your mechanic doesn't have to tighten your belts anymore (and you don't have to tighten your own belt to afford auto repairs). Rule of thumb: if the belt is loose, have it inspected or replaced.

A Tale of Two [or more] Belts

Back in the 1970s, most cars used somewhere in the range of three to five different belts to drive the engine's various components. These days, most cars feature one multi-functioning serpentine belt. Always found at the front of the engine, this multi-tasking wonder works the alternator, power steering, water pump, air pump and air conditioning.

Inside the Car

There are problems that can be detected inside the car while you're driving, such as wind noise or dashboard rattling. These are things that you might be able to diagnose—and even fix—by yourself.

The hole business

Wind noise can drive you crazy. You roll up every window and close every vent trying to put an end to that annoying whistle. You've checked all the doors, but it won't go away. Somewhere there's a hole. It could be that a rust problem has led to a hole in the car's sheet metal, and the wind's blowing right over it, like blowing across the top of a bottle. Or the molding around the door may have become frayed or loose, or even ripped. This one's easy to assess by yourself. Just slip a piece of paper between the molding and the door. Close the door and see if the paper comes out easily. If it does, then you've found your problem.

I think you may have a screw loose

Dash rattling is also a fun one for the do-it-yourselfer. If your dashboard is shakin' an' a-rattlin', just get a screwdriver, or a small socket set, and start twisting, turning and tightening any loose screw, nut or bolt that you can find. You'd be surprised how easy this is: one quarter-inch turn could be enough to fix the problem. It could be that your glove box door is misaligned. Or it could be that there is no problem: in a new car—or a new house—some settling does occur. Still, it couldn't hurt to keep checking for loose screws.

Other loose parts might go flap flap flap, or bang bang bang, like a loose shutter. Again, if this is what you hear, all it takes is a quick look around. Walk around the car. Look for something loose, something barely hanging on, like loose moldings or **mud flaps**, **splash shields** or **air dams**, **deflectors** or **tailpipes**. Grab anything that moves, anything that you think might have become free-moving. Shake the tailpipe. Wiggle the mud flaps. Get out your trusty screwdriver and tighten any screws you think might have come loose. Then take the car out for a test drive to see if you've solved the problem.

A test drive, by the way, can be the best way to diagnose car trouble. And a second set of ears couldn't hurt. If we're talking about a problem that occurs only on the road, take the car out for a drive, with someone from the garage, if possible. Sometimes words are not enough, and the mechanic has to hear for herself what the problem might be. As the saying goes, two heads (and thus four ears) are better than one. Take a friend for a drive and have him listen for the noise that you've been hearing. But have him sit in the back seat on the passenger side; sometimes the noise sounds like it might be coming from the front of the car when it's actually coming from somewhere toward the back. You can even keep a written journal of an intermittent problem. Keep track of what you're hearing, when you're hearing it, where you're hearing it. It's a great way to tell your mechanic exactly what you think might be wrong with your car, like drawing a road map.

Look carefully, though. You might think you hear a noise that indicates a problem where there isn't one. Rattling or clunking in the trunk, for example, might just be empty pop cans, or a child's toy that's been left in the car and has fallen into the wheel well. Sometimes your car jack becomes loose in its storage hub. Wouldn't you hate to bring your car into the garage only to be told that the source of your problem was an empty windshield washer container being tossed around the trunk?

Only the Nose Knows

Your sense of smell can also be an effective tool in diagnosing potential problems. An oily smell can mean that your engine oil cap is missing or that a gasket is leaking. A smell like burning rope could indicate a slipping clutch, binding brakes or a parking brake that's been left on. Gas smells can point to an overfull or leaking fuel tank, a leaky fuel pump or a flooded carburetor.

Other Problems That You Can Feel

There are other problems that don't come with sounds or vibrations, but you can "feel" them, like a body lean, for instance. When you turn a corner and you feel the car leaning heavily to one side, or even tilting, you've got a suspension problem. You feel this in big old American cars with what I call soft or mushy suspension, like old Cadillacs and Chevy Caprices.

Wonky suspension can cause what's called "dog-tracking," because your car will imitate what a dog does when it runs on a diagonal. This usually indicates a problem with alignment. If this happens, you'll feel as if your car isn't stable on the road, doesn't hold the road properly, and drives a little off-kilter. A suspension problem could also be the cause of misalignment, and might be accompanied by a knock or a creak.

Enlightenment

I've already emphasized the importance of reading your owner's manual. It should be right there in the glove box, next to your gloves and this book. But how often do you look at it? You should read through it at least once, when you take your new baby home. The manual has everything you need to know about your specific car, and being familiar with it will only help you, *especially* if you've got this book as a companion.

One of the first pages in the manual should explain all the dashboard lights that come on when you start the car, the same ones that might stay on, or flash, if there is a problem. And since we're talking about diagnosing car trouble on your own, it would be a good idea to understand these lights. They're called **diagnostic lights**, or warning lights, and that's what they're there for. For example, if your OD (overdrive) light or your electronic suspension light flashes, that could indicate that the computer for either of those circuits has found a problem and is flashing a diagnostic code. In other words, your car has diagnosed itself. These dashboard lights come on briefly when you turn the key in the ignition. But how many of us really pay attention to them? Well, I do, but then I'm a mechanic. When these lights come on briefly they're doing a system check, making sure all systems are go before you get going. Once you understand these lights, you'll know if there's a problem.

Okay, so you found a problem, you figured out what it was and you went through the process of having it repaired under your watchful eye. You're not done yet. The last step in the diagnostic process is another test drive, preferably with the mechanic. Insist on it, but do it before you pay the bill. You want to make sure the problem has been solved. Hopefully, if you've chosen the right mechanic, he'll understand and won't mind the drive, or the break from the garage.

But what makes a good mechanic, and where do you find one? Ah, I'm glad you asked. Please read on.

5

Tips and Tricks of the Trade: Talking to Your Mechanic

Okay, so now that you know how to diagnose your own car trouble, you're more of an armchair mechanic than a clueless one. Good thing you bought this book. But what will you do with your newfound knowledge? Now that you can zero in on what you think might be wrong with your car, whom do you take it to for repairs? As I said in the last chapter, your mechanic must be someone you trust. Don't worry, there are ways to go about finding the right garage and the right mechanic.

Once you've found Mr. or Ms Right you need to develop a good relationship with him or her. In this chapter we'll talk about how to find a garage where you'd feel comfortable bringing your car. I'll tell you how to communicate with your mechanic, what to say, what not to say and, perhaps most importantly, how to protect yourself, your car and your wallet.

You Can't Judge a Book by Its Cover. But a Garage?

Finding the right garage is like searching for the Northwest Passage, except now you get to talk to other "explorers" who have, to mix metaphors, been down that road. Say you've just moved into a new neighborhood and you need to have your car serviced. Where do you start? Word of mouth is a good first step. Ask around. Talk to your new neighbors, or a colleague at work. Then go ahead and follow up on those recommendations.

But once you find a garage, don't just go in and leave your car with the first grease monkey you meet. Do a drive-by and see what the place looks like from the outside. Does it look like the kind of place you'd feel comfortable leaving your car? Go on in and have a look around. Is it clean? Is it well painted and presentable? These aren't normally the kinds of questions you'd expect to ask about a garage, but you'd be surprised how important it is to find a garage that's well cared for. A clean garage should indicate that its mechanics would probably give your car the same consideration they've given their own shop. If you don't like the look of the place, and your gut tells you not to leave your car there, move on.

A bad garage has probably developed a reputation. Everybody knows about a bad garage, either because they've had a bad experience there themselves or because they know someone who has. The drive-by works in this case, too. A run-down, dirty place with a cluttered junkyard out back and parts strewn all over the place probably isn't the best place to take your car.

Still, you might be inclined to get past the veneer and give the place a chance. Did you like the way the staff treated you when you walked in? How are they treating your car? If you suspect they're taking out their frustrations on it, you probably don't want to leave your car in their hands. Remember, though, that your relationship with your mechanic is a two-way street; you choose to go to him, presumably, because you feel he's a professional and he knows his job. Treat him with the same respect you expect him to show you and your car. Not that he'll mistreat your car if you're nasty. But maybe being nice will get your car better service faster.

Meet the Parents: Trusting Your Baby to a New Guy

If you like the look of the place, then it's time to break the ice. Introduce yourself. Say, "Hi, I'm Ms Smith. I've just moved into the neighborhood, and I'm looking for a mechanic." See how you're received, and don't be afraid to ask the mechanic the kinds of questions you might ask your daughter's boyfriend: "What kind of work do you do? How long have you been in the business? Is the guy behind the counter the owner of the shop?" Sometimes, if the owner also works at the counter, it shows that he takes a special interest in the customers and is concerned about the kind of service they receive. Take the tummy test: what does your gut tell you? Are you beginning to grow more comfortable with your surroundings? This just might be the place for you and your car.

You can also check with the American Automobile Association (AAA) or the Canadian Automobile Association (CAA) or even the Better Business Bureau (see Resources). Some businesses will even display a plaque that says they are recognized by either one or all of these organizations.

Still not completely happy? Test the place out. Request a small job, a simple oil change, for instance, and see how you and your car are handled. Will they let you watch? Can you talk to the mechanic? What would you say to him?

Talking to Your Mechanic: Don't Be Embarrassed

When Viagra hit pharmacy shelves there was a fabulous television commercial in which a guy sat in his doctor's examining room, dog-faced, in his socks and boxers. You knew that something was on his mind. But when his doctor asked him if there was anything else he wanted to talk about, he masked his anxiety with a touch of false bravado and shook his head "no." The commercial emphasized the importance of talking to your doctor openly.

It's the same thing with auto mechanics. Some drivers are afraid to talk to their mechanic about everything that might be wrong with their car, either because they don't know very much about cars and don't want to look stupid, or because they think a mechanic will charge them for things that don't need fixing. You should be open with your mechanic. In Chapter 4, I mentioned how important trust is, and how dangerous it is to simply toss him the keys. You know your car. And after reading the previous chapters, you should know your tocs from your knocks, and your tics from your clicks. You're more familiar with your car and how it works than you were before you picked up this book in the bookstore, right? The truth is, you're completely capable of explaining in your own way what you think might be wrong with your car, and your mechanic will understand you—if you are clear.

Turn your head and cough

The first time you see a new doctor she'll probably give you a complete physical checkup. She'll check your blood pressure and listen to your heart in order to get an idea of the overall state of your health. By talking with you openly she'll get a better sense of what she's dealing with. A mechanic will do the same thing. After speaking with you, she'll give your car the once-over, checking the fuel pressure and listening to the engine. The main difference between a doctor and a mechanic is that a doctor only ever has to deal with two basic models, male and female. A mechanic gets 200 new models a year. And as far as I know, mechanics don't golf on Wednesdays.

Once you've found a garage and a mechanic you like, you can get into the kinds of conversations we talked about in Chapter 4, that ritual dance of charades and sounds that brings her closer to an understanding of why you're in her garage.

How to Get the Best Price

This is where it all counts. If you can use your newly acquired knowledge to save yourself some bucks, then you've got gold.

Shops charge in different ways. Some charge by the hour, and however long it takes to fix your car, that's how long it takes. It's the labor costs that'll getcha in the end. Other shops might charge a flat rate per job regardless of how long it takes, which could work out in the customer's favor. Your garage might charge you a flat rate for a repair job based on an *estimated hourly rate* of how long it should normally take to do that job, plus parts and labor, of course. They might budget an hour to repair your cooling system, for example. Based on that, they might charge $75 to service the cooling system. That's how much it should cost whether it takes them 50 minutes or an hour and a half. In these cases, your mechanic is probably following what's called a "labor guide." Some aftermarket data suppliers, like Chilton, Mitchell or Alldata, publish such labor guides. Mechanics sometimes rely on them for technical information, in the same way that a surgeon might consult a guide on surgical procedures to see how long things normally takes and, based on that, how much to charge the patient, er, customer.

Dealerships have their own guides. Because they have the specialized knowledge and the proper tools, they should be able to do a specific repair job in less time than it would take the mechanics at an independent garage. However, specialized knowledge and tools cost money too, so the price of a certain job will probably vary greatly depending on whether you get it done at the garage or the dealership. Furthermore, certain repairs might still be under warranty depending on the age of your car.

Just to give you an idea of what your average mechanic is up against, consider his overhead costs. Most mechanics are always updating and investing in their toolboxes to make sure they're equipped with all the latest tools necessary to fix your car and all the new models that come out every year. Indeed, when a manufacturer comes out with a new part, a mechanic often needs to buy a specific tool to repair that part. That's the kind of thing he'll take into account when deciding how much to charge.

My momma told me ya better shop around

So how do you make sure you're getting the best possible price for a repair job? A lazy car owner might end up paying an unnecessarily high price for a job if all he does is leave his car with the first clean garage he finds. You've got to do the footwork. Again, don't just toss the mechanic your keys. Get an estimate on a job and then hit the pavement. Take the estimate away with you and call around to or visit other garages. Get a second opinion, and see if you can get the job done more cheaply somewhere else. But don't stop there. Take your new estimate back to the first guy and see if he'll either match the new price or go even lower. This is a good policy when shopping for anything, by the way, not just car repairs. Keep in mind, though, that cheapest isn't always best. Use your judgment. If the shop is offering you a rock-bottom price, but you don't trust the look or feel of the place, it may be better to pay a little more for some peace of mind.

It's a tough call: sometimes a mechanic is actually looking out for your best interests, which might include trying to save you money. We're selfless that way...and we'd love to have you come back to our place again, so we want to make sure you're satisfied. But you have to think things through, as well. Say you need a timing belt, but on your car the timing belt also drives the water pump. Your mechanic might recommend that you change the water pump and the **oil seals** along with the belt. You might feel that's unnecessary, mainly because you don't want to pay all that money right now. Think about it, though,

Lisa's Tip
Here's another way to save money. If you can live without your car for a few days, ask your mechanic if you can leave it at the garage for her do the repairs bit by bit when she can find the time. She can use your car as a filler job if a client cancels an appointment, or if she finds some extra time here and there. You could save on labor.

because your mechanic just might be right. If all you fix is the belt, and then six months later the water pump goes, you'll end up having the whole job done all over again, which will cost you more in the end. In certain cases it might seem like we're scamming you by trying to get you to fix something that ain't broke. But we might really be trying to save you trouble down the road. It's sometimes smarter to do a whole job while you're there at the garage, especially if it's only a question of paying for the part, with the bulk of the labor already being done.

Grouping repairs together saves on labor. But you can also try bargaining with your mechanic. Mechanics in some small independent places will do it. If you have a lot of repairs, or a big job, see what happens if you ask for a discount on the parts (mark-up value). You could try to bargain on the labor, too, but start with the parts.

Specialists and generalists

Some car owners become comfortable with a mechanic and only ever go to the one guy, whether it's for regular maintenance or special jobs such as mufflers or brakes. But there are many specialty shops out there that only do one kind of job, such as fixing and replacing mufflers or brakes. These guys are specialists, so you know they do these specific jobs right. Your corner mechanic is more like a GP. I know, I know: again with the medical references. But the principle really is the same. There are also transmission and differential specialists, engine rebuilding specialists, and body shops.

Your corner mechanic can probably get all of these things done for you if you ask him to, or if you just don't have the time or the inclination to shop around for a specialist. He doesn't want to lose you as a customer, so he'll take your job. But since he's a generalist, he might not have the specific tools or know-how for certain jobs. He might not even want to occupy one of his bays with a big-ticket job, so he may outsource the job to someone else. But that won't save you any money, if that's your goal. But you might save money if you do the footwork. First, just get out there and find a specialist. Then get estimates, haggle, shop around, and you might be able to save yourself some dough.

Checklist Bargain Shopping

If you're looking to get the best price possible for your repair, consider the following:

✔ Shop around (don't take the word of one garage as gospel).
✔ Get estimates (they make great ammunition when it comes to the next step).
✔ Haggle (you'd be surprised at how much is negotiable).
✔ Hire a specialist (he may know the car better and take less time to do the repair).
✔ Leave your vehicle at the shop (you might be able to work out a deal if you can leave your car longer and your mechanic can work on your job around others).

Mechanical Faux Pas: What Not to Say

Remember that regardless of how thorough this book has been so far, you are not a mechanic. Trying to save yourself some bucks on a diagnostic test is not always the best thing for your car. Yes, you do want to be able to diagnose your own car trouble, but not so that you can tell your mechanic what to do and how to do it. You simply want a bit of control over what happens to your car.

If you're telling your mechanic to change a part because you don't trust his professional judgment, then you're in the wrong garage. Some people just don't trust mechanics. If you're that type, you might be in for some problems. If you tell a mechanic that your car doesn't start and that he should change the alternator, he may go ahead and change it, just because you said so. But that might not have been the problem, and your car still might not start after the work is done. That's your fault. Too many customers are unwilling to pay for the time and labor it takes to check their car. If you don't want to give away all your symptoms, or trust in the mechanic's knowledge and abilities, then you're going to cost yourself more money in the long run.

When it comes to car repairs and saving money, the other option is to do the repairs yourself. If you wouldn't mind tinkering under the hood a bit, the next chapter provides a do-it-yourself guide. Go and get your coveralls. It's time to roll up your sleeves and have some fun.

Gettin' Down and Dirty: Lisa's Do-It-Yourself Guide

Okay, so you've made the transition from clueless mechanic to armchair mechanic. But you won't do your car any good from the comfort of your living room. So let's get you up out of that chair, into some coveralls, and out into the garage. It's a Saturday afternoon, and you've always wanted to tinker under the hood of your car. Well, who hasn't? It's the reason you bought this book, right? So let's get to it.

At this point you should at least have taken a peek inside your car's owner's manual. Remember the owner's manual? Reading the darned thing is the one thing almost all car owners neglect to do, when it's the first thing they ought to do once they get their new baby home. Yours is probably still sitting there in the plastic envelope your dealer provides. Go and get it, and put it in your bathroom. That's the best place for it; you'll never be without something to read, and it's the one place you're sure not to be disturbed. And, who knows, you might find the rest of your family has been flipping through it, too. The more all of you know about the family car, the better.

Getting Acquainted with Your Car

I can't stress enough how important it is to review your owner's manual. It will tell you everything you need to know about your car. Once you've had a chance to read it, go outside and give your car the once-over. Get acquainted with the engine. Find all your fuse boxes. Have a look at where the spare tire is kept. You can even bookmark certain sections of the manual with Post-it® Notes or tag various engine parts with masking tape. This might seem elementary, but I've seen people pour windshield washer fluid into the antifreeze reservoir, and vice versa. Tag things so you know where to find them. Your mechanic will be impressed.

I Can Do It All by Myself

If you're the owner of a new car, then you'll probably see your dealer for most of your repairs and regular maintenance. And even if you're driving a secondhand clunker, there are certain things you'll need a mechanic to do. But there is no greater feeling for a car owner of any kind than the satisfaction of knowing he's been able to make at least some minor repairs or take care

Save Those Receipts!

If you are going to do some of your own repairs, like oil changes, make sure to keep a careful record of the work that you do and when you do it. Make note of the mileage, and keep receipts for the new parts that you buy, including the oil filter and the oil itself. In some cases, failure to produce this information can void your warranty. Even if that's not the case, if you ever want to sell your car, the potential new owner will appreciate the records.

of some regular maintenance by himself. This section is the do-it-yourself guide for those of you who want to get dirty. I'll tell you how to check your tire pressure, how to change lightbulbs and fuses, and even how to change the oil. But before we get started there are a few things you need to know.

Safety First

This rule applies just as much in your driveway or garage as it does on the road. Always be mindful of your safety and of the safety of those around you whenever you play mechanic. You'll be handling harmful chemicals, sharp tools and heavy parts. Safety ought to be your first and last thought when you're working on your own car.

Keep a pair of gloves on hand. Mechanics these days use gloves made from neoprene, a synthetic rubber that's more resistant to oil. You can also use an old pair of dishwashing gloves. Your gloves should protect you against dirt and contamination. Many of the materials you'll be working with, such as dirty motor oil, can be carcinogenic.

Remember to remove all jewellery, including your wedding band. Rings, bracelets and necklaces can get caught on moving parts or even conduct electricity (but put your wedding band back on when you're done; you don't want your partner to think you've been sneakin' around). Wear tight-fitting clothes and tie up your hair if it's long. I learned firsthand the importance of tying back my pretty blonde locks. Once, as a young mechanics student, I was working under a car and my hair got caught under the wheels of a creeper (that's the square skateboard-looking thing you lie on to get under a car). A spark from my blowtorch flew into my hair and threatened to light up my head like I was Michael Jackson in a Pepsi commercial. Now I always tie it up in a braid or tuck it under a baseball cap. You should see how sexy I look when I take off the cap and shake out my hair. But I digress.

Crude Work: Changing the Oil

Of all the jobs in this section, the one that will make you feel most like a mechanic is changing the oil. It's probably the biggest, and most important, of the do-it-yourself jobs. It's crucial to the upkeep of your engine and thus prolongs the life of your car. It's also relatively easy. Anyone can do it, and everyone should try it at least once just for the experience.

But don't stop at a simple oil change. Once you've got the costume on, you may as well play the part to the hilt. When you have your oil changed at the garage, the mechanic usually goes through a checklist, giving your car a 10-, 15- or sometimes even a 40-point inspection, topping up fluids and checking the tire pressure. There's no reason you can't do the same thing. So before you change your own oil, make a list: what is it you want to accomplish? I'll tell you how to take advantage of the time it takes to do an oil change and use it to give your car a bit of a checkup.

Checklist Tools of the trade

Here's everything you'll need to do an oil change:

- ✔ Gloves (neoprene or old dishwashing gloves)
- ✔ Goggles or safety glasses
- ✔ Clean rags
- ✔ A drain pan that will hold at least 1.5 gallons (5 l)
- ✔ New oil filter
- ✔ 1–1.5 gallons (4–5 l) oil
- ✔ A shallow pan with kitty litter to absorb spillage
- ✔ A filter wrench/tool (ask someone at the auto shop, you'll probably need one specific to your engine)
- ✔ The right size wrench for your drain plug
- ✔ A jack and a set of jack stands

A note about jacks and jack stands: The little jack that comes with your car is meant for changing a spare tire, a relatively simple procedure that can be done at the side of the road. But that's all it was intended for. It's not good enough if you're planning on crawling underneath the car. Remember that your car literally weighs a ton. Cinder blocks will not do, either; they are meant for building foundations, not for jacking up cars—especially not if you're going to be lying underneath them. Most auto centers sell a box kit that contains a hydraulic jack with two jack stands. That's the *only* thing that'll do. And two jack stands are all you'll need to secure the car if all you're doing is a front oil change.

Getting started

Before you jack up the car make sure the handbrake is engaged. Never jack up a car without putting on the handbrake, regardless of whether your car's standard or automatic. (You need to lock the wheels in place, and you shouldn't rely on your transmission to do the trick.)

You need to make sure your car stays securely in one place and doesn't roll off the jack stands, so you'll need something to block the wheels. The last time you were on an airplane waiting for takeoff, did you notice the technicians taking something out from under the wheels just before the plane rolled down the runway? Those are special blocks that help keep the plane in one place until the pilot is absolutely certain he's ready for takeoff. You can make a small set for your car. Get a 4-foot length of 4 x 4 inch (10 cm x 10 cm) lumber. Cut the wood into four angled pieces, to use under each wheel. Bolt sets of two pieces of wood together with a piece of chain, and now you have your own custom-made wheel blockers. You can hang those up in your garage and take them down any time you need to keep your car from rolling.

For obvious reasons, it's always best to work on a cold car. It's tough to handle hot auto parts; hot fluids can scald you. That being said, consider also that cool engine oil thickens slightly, and once your engine has had a chance to cool, oil will have settled into all the little gullies and valleys around the engine. In other words, not all of it will have dripped down into the oil pan. Remember that the oil pan is both the starting point and end point of the maze that is your engine. When you start your car, the oil is drawn up out of the pan, flows through the engine, and flows back down into the pan, where it settles when you turn off your car (Fig. 1). When you change the oil, it's the pan that you empty, and it would indeed be logical to assume that all the oil has drained down into it. But that's not the case. So, although it is safer to work on a cold car, it's not a bad idea to have your car idle, just for a few minutes, to warm the oil so that it thins just enough to drain better. In fact, if you know you need to pick up tools and parts, and the auto shop's not very far away, drive there and back just before you do the oil change. That'll give your car a chance to warm up just enough so that you can change the oil, but the car won't get so hot that you'll injure yourself.

A complete oil change includes changing the oil filter and changing the oil. If you change just the filter, you'll be left with oil that is still dirty. If you change just the oil and not the filter, then your filter's still dirty, and what's the point of filtering clean oil through dirt?

Getting down to it

Okay, you've got everything you need, and now you're ready to start. First, let's find the best location to jack up your car safely. That means two things: you want to find the best place on the body of your car to place your jack and jack stands, and you want to find the best, and safest, location either in your driveway or in your garage to do the job. For obvious reasons, you want to do this on a flat surface. You don't want your car rolling away or falling off the jack stands while you're underneath it. So don't use your driveway if it slopes.

It might be best to put your jack and jack stands on a sheet of wood under your car. In case you're working on asphalt, the wood will save you from a danger you may not even have known existed. Asphalt gets hot in the sun and can melt, or at least soften. Your jacks can sink so deep into the asphalt that you can get pinned under the car. This happened to me. Now, I know what you must be thinking: first the blowtorched hair, and now this. Well, believe me when I tell you that I was not always the mechanical genius I am today.

When I was in shop class in high school, for example, I was taking spare parts from a classmate's car (it's okay; he told me

Lisa's Tip
Don't use bricks to support your car. They can crumble under the car's weight and leave you pinned underneath.

I could). I jacked up the car properly and slid underneath on a creeper (this time with my hair tucked safely under my cap). But it was a hot day and I was under the car for a long time, working on an asphalt surface. The car began to sink so gradually that I didn't notice. Before I knew it, I was pinned! I called for help, and thankfully someone heard me and came to jack the car up off my chest. But if I'd been there long enough the car would have sunk low enough to squeeze the breath right out of me. *That's why it's a good idea to have someone with you when you're doing this type of job.* Just to be on the safe side, then, slide a sheet of wood under the jack stand before you put the jack in place.

You'll need three spots for your jack and the jack stands, and your mechanic can probably help you with that. Most cars have a spot on the side just behind the wheel that's solid enough to accommodate a jack. Jack up the car, and set your stands underneath for support. Not sure if it's solid? Test it. Give your car a shove or a bit of a body check. As long as it's good and solid, and you're sure you're not in any danger of being pinned under the car, you're ready to get underneath.

Wait! Take a second to put your car keys in your pocket. The last thing you want is for somebody to come along and turn on the ignition when you're under the car. Are the keys in the ignition? Go get 'em and put 'em in your pocket until the job's done. Now go ahead and slide underneath the car.

First, locate the engine. I assume you know where it is after my fine description in Chapter 1. But remember that the engine and the transmission are bolted together, and the whole thing together might seem, at least at first, as convoluted as your cerebral cortex. So when I say "locate the engine" I mean take a good look at it, with your owner's manual in your hand, and try to find where everything is, starting with the oil pan. Keep in mind, though, that everything will look different when you're looking up—rather than down—at it.

Now find the oil filter, because you're going to change your filter first. Once you've located the filter, unscrew it counter-clockwise.

Once you've removed the old filter, take a couple of clean rags and clean the area around the oil filter housing. You want to make sure it's clean in order to ensure a proper seal once you put a new filter on. Also, the rubber gasket that helps make a proper seal might be stuck inside the housing. If it's left in there it will compromise a new seal. There is nothing worse than spending all your money on fresh oil only to start the engine and watch it all come spewing out the underside of the car.

Before you install the new filter, compare it to the old one. Make sure, in other words, that you've got the right kind of fil-

The Oil Change

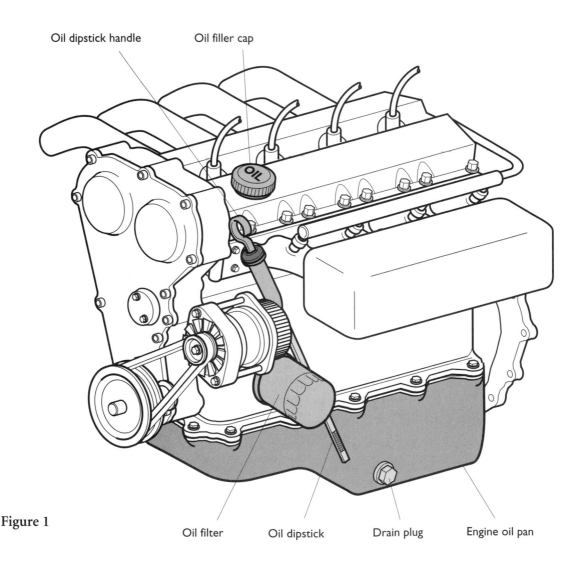

Oil dipstick handle   Oil filler cap

Oil filter   Oil dipstick   Drain plug   Engine oil pan

Figure 1

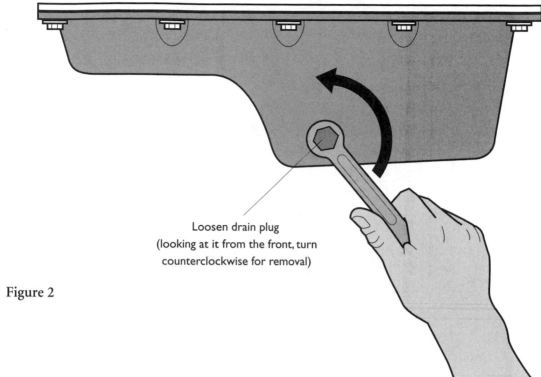

Loosen drain plug
(looking at it from the front, turn
counterclockwise for removal)

Figure 2

ter. Do they look the same? If you poke your finger into the
threaded hole, does it go the same distance? Do the threads
look the same? Your first oil change could be nerve-racking,
especially if you're ever so slightly obsessive-compulsive. You
just want to make sure all the parts are the right ones. If you've
got the wrong filter or a bad seal, you'll leak oil all over the
place—and with no oil to lubricate all the moving parts, you
could blow your engine—and your cool, when you see the
mess! Don't put the new filter on just yet; you want to have a
bit of air flowing through the system to help push the old oil
out. So just put the new filter up on top of the engine, next to
where it goes.

Now it's time to drain the oil. Find the oil pan and look for
a bolt at the very bottom (Fig. 2). That's what plugs the oil pan
drain hole. Have your drain pan ready. Place it just slightly in
front of the drain plug, because the first bit of oil will flow out-
ward (Fig. 3). Be prepared: Chances are you're going to make a
hell of mess your first time out. But that's part of the fun.

Loosen the bolt, hold onto it, and then get out of the way.

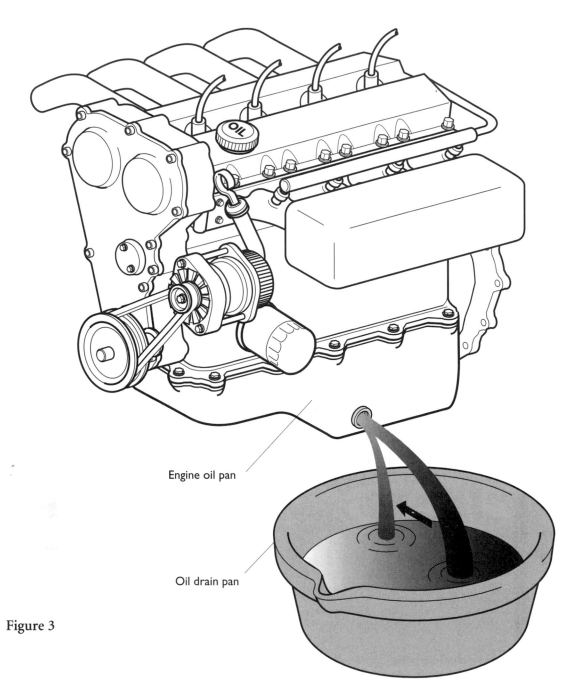

Engine oil pan

Oil drain pan

Figure 3

The pressure of the draining oil will push against the drain plug, and if you don't have a good grip on it, you'll lose it. Hold onto it until you can slide out of the way a bit.

Let the oil drain completely. It starts with a quick burst where it's thick, which is why you've placed the drain pan for-

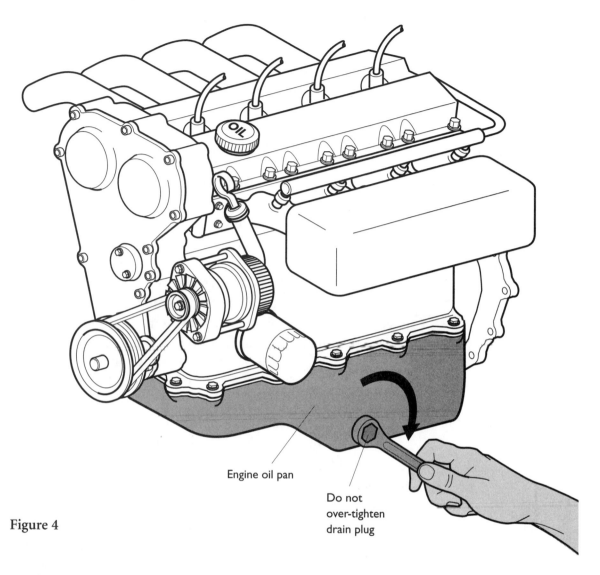

Figure 4

Engine oil pan

Do not
over-tighten
drain plug

ward a bit. You can move it back as the flow slows to a steady stream. Let it drain until there are only a few droplets. This will likely take five to seven minutes, so while that's happening you can go around the top end of the car. Check the air filter. Check the power-steering fluid. You can also check the tire pressure, even if your car is jacked up. This is exactly what your mechanic would do. Use the time while the oil drains to give your car the once-over. Check for loose moldings, and top up the windshield washer fluid. Have a notepad handy, jotting down anything you think might need to be looked at by a mechanic.

By now your oil should be drained. Replace the drain plug. You might have to change the gasket if you have the type of drain plug whose gasket needs to be changed. Some gaskets are little rings of copper, some are plastic and some are a paper-rubber compound. Some drain plugs are disposable. But basically, in these models, the bolt and the gasket are made as one piece. You use these a couple of times, then you replace the whole thing.

Reinstall the bolt by using your fingers at first, then tighten it up with your wrench. How tight should it be? That's tough to say, because it comes down to experience. As a general guideline, once the bolt is snug, give it another quarter turn just to be sure. (Fig. 4).

Let's not forget the new filter. The reason you put it on top is because it's easy to forget. Spread a drop of clean oil along the gasket (the sticky moisture will ensure a good tight seal) and replace the filter. Once again, screw on the filter by hand, finger-tight, and then snug it up with your tool, one last turn-and-a-half after it's snug. You don't need it to be super-tight; just make sure that you've got a good seal and that you or your mechanic won't have trouble loosening it the next time.

You've drained the oil and put on a new, clean filter. Now you can add new oil. Depending on the make of your car, you may or may not need a funnel. Make sure you're adding the right amount. Your car probably takes about 1–1.5 gallons (4–5 l) of oil. Check your owner's manual. Start with 1 gallon (4 l), then check the oil as you might do during a fill-up at the gas station. Take out the **dipstick**, wipe it off, then stick it back in, then pull it back out and have a look at it. If you still need a bit of oil, go ahead and top it up. A bit less than full is fine for now; just make sure you don't overfill it.

Okay, you're done. Good job! Now before you let the car down, start 'er up to make sure there are no leaks. The oil filter should fill up, and the oil should begin to flow through the engine. As long as there are no leaks, you can let the car down. At this point the oil's had time to drain. Check the dipstick again to see if you need to top it up, but remember not to put in too much.

If you've got a mess on the ground, your engine is clacking,

Lisa's Tip
Put the drain plug you removed next to the tool you used; that way you'll know where to find it later.

Recycling Your Used Oil

The Environmental Protection Agency estimates that, in the U.S. alone, 200 million gallons (757 million liters) of used motor oil is being dumped on the ground, tossed in the trash or poured down sewers and drains. Just 1 gallon (4 l) has the potential to contaminate a million gallons of drinking water and threaten a variety of aquatic life. To safely and properly dispose of your used oil, pour it into a clean, leakproof container with a screw-on top. (Make sure not to put it in a container that's held household chemicals, such as bleach.) Take the container to your local used oil collection center. If your community doesn't have one, check with a nearby service center or repair shop.

or your dashboard oil light is on, you know there is a problem. Turn off the car, and retrace your steps to see if you can figure out what went wrong.

While you're at it...

Remember that the oil change gives you the opportunity to take care of some other things. While you're at it, go ahead and change the air filter, just like the mechanics at a garage would do. Make that part of the routine. Granted, the garage wants to sell you a new air filter, but you do want to make sure you haven't sucked anything up into the air filter that might block it.

As long as you've got your head under the hood of your car, you might as well check your fluids. By that I mean all the fluids that you can check visually, seeing the levels on their respective reservoirs. Top them up if you need to, or, if they're fluids that should be changed only by professionals, such as brake fluid, just make a note of it, and have them changed or topped up at the garage later on. You can take a marker and highlight the "full" line on the brake-fluid reservoir on the master cylinder, because it's usually hard to see. Shaking the

fluid reservoir to see the fluid move around a bit can sometimes help. Also check the power-steering fluid and the coolant,
always making sure the engine is cool, because you don't want
to get burned. The only fluid you can't check while the car is up
on jacks is the transmission fluid, so that one will have to wait
until your car is back down on level ground.

Fuse Boxes

Cars today are packed with modern conveniences, most of
which are electric. There are more **fuses** in a car than ever
before, so cars now come with a few different fuse boxes. Again,
flip through the owner's manual, find out where the fuse boxes
are, and learn what kinds of fuses you'll need for your car's
electrical appliances. Some day you might find yourself in a
position in which you'll have to change a fuse yourself. You
don't want to be caught in the rain with wipers that don't work
because a fuse has blown.

Changing Lightbulbs

Your owner's manual will tell you how to change the **lightbulbs**
for your particular car, but the procedure's pretty simple; in
fact, it's probably too simple to be called a procedure.

Before replacing any bulb, remember to disconnect the circuit in question (this is a good rule when doing any kind of
electrical work, even in the home). Always use the same type of
bulb as the one you're replacing. Some dealers recommend that
you keep spare bulbs with you at all times. (I can't stand it
when a car coming at me has a burned-out bulb and the driver's got his high beams on to compensate because he couldn't
be bothered to have the bulb changed.) You'll need bulbs for
the headlights, parking lights, brake lights and turn signals.
Those are the basics. Your car might also call for other types of
bulbs, such as fog lights and license plate lights.

Some vehicles require you to remove the whole headlight casing (the housing that contains the bulb) to change the bulb itself. However, most headlights have a release lever that allows you to slip out the headlight bulb easily. There is probably a wire, or wires, that you'll have to disconnect before pulling out the old bulb, as well as a release tab that holds the bulb in place. Always use a tissue or a cloth when installing a new bulb, especially with halogens; oil from your fingertips can damage the bulb and dull the reflector surface. Once you've got the new bulb in place, just do everything in reverse order, folding the protective tab over the bulb, reconnecting the wire and replacing the casing. The procedure for replacing the taillights should be similar. You might need some tools, probably a screwdriver, to replace some of the other bulbs. Again, consult your owner's manual.

Changing Wipers

Changing **wipers** used to be the easiest thing in the world to do. But at some point in the last 10 years or so it has become rather complicated. This job is not for the faint of heart. Some newer models have even the most seasoned mechanics swearin' up a blue streak because they can't get the damn wiper blade off. So, for what it's worth, here's how it's done.

You'll need a small blanket or towel. You see, a wiper arm, the medal rod a wiper blade is attached to, has a spring in it to keep constant pressure against your windshield. When you change a wiper blade, you'll have to lift up the arm. Most of the time, when you lift up the arm it stays up. But sometimes, because of the spring, it snaps back down against your windshield and could crack it, hence the protective blanket. Lay it against the windshield so that if the arm snaps back you've got some padding protecting the glass.

Lift up the wiper arms. Take your new blades out of the package and compare them with the ones you are replacing. Have a look at all the extra pieces in the package. Take everything out and put it all in front of you along with the packaged instructions. Now the fun begins.

Grasp the blade and find the lock tab. Press firmly and slide the wiper blade back. This should release the blade, although it might take a bit of effort. Once the blade is removed, compare the adapter with the ones that came with the new blades. Slide on the new blade, working in the reverse order. There. You're done. And if you're not, start again. You'll get it eventually.

It'll All Come out in the Wash

All of us wash our cars. You wouldn't think you'd need instructions on how to do this properly. But then again, even shampoo bottles come with directions. You'd be surprised what kind of damage you can do to your car's finish if you don't use the right soap and the right technique, and if you don't dry your car properly. So, for the record, here's how to wash your car.

Lather. Rinse. Repeat.

Using cold water, soak the car thoroughly, from the top down, to loosen up the dirt. Oh, and no matter what you've been told, don't use dish soap—unless you want to strip all the wax off your car. That's what professional car detailers do, by the way: they take off your old finish and redo it completely. But that's a huge, expensive job. If all you want to do is wash your car on a sunny Saturday afternoon, then keep it simple. Any car wash product will do, as long as it is indeed intended for washing your car and not your china. And never wash a car in direct sunlight, because you'll end up baking the water and the soap into your finish.

You'll need a proper sponge or a car wash mitt and a deep bucket. Any dirt collected on the sponge or mitt will sink to the bottom of the bucket as you wash, and the cleaner water will stay on top.

Now that you've soaked your car down, soap it up. Do a section at a time. Start with the roof, then rinse it down. Continue on to the front windshield, wipers and wiper arms, then rinse. Move on to all the windows, then rinse. You get the picture. Save the wheels for last, but don't use the car mitt on the wheels. The brake dust, grease and goop caked onto the wheels will get imbedded in the glove and spoil it. Use an old sponge for the wheels.

There really is a proper drying technique, by the way. Take a close look at your nice clean car on a sunny day. Do you notice any circular, spiderweb-looking scratches on the hood of the car? That's from using the wrong kind of towel or rag to dry your car. A chamois is best because it won't leave any marks.

Checklist The Dos and Don'ts of Car Washing

If you've read the section about washing your car, you know it isn't as simple as throwing on some soap and water and calling it good. Here's a quick list of dos and don'ts:

✔ Don't wash your car in direct sunlight (you'll bake on the soap and ruin your finish).
✔ Don't use dish soap (it will strip off your wax).
✔ Don't use hot water (it can cause water droplets to form, creating a spotty finish).
✔ Do use clean mitts and chamois (dirty ones contain dirt particles that can scratch your finish).
✔ Do use a deep bucket (dirt and grime will sink to the bottom, where your mitt won't pick it up).

Spit and polish

After you're done you may find your car is covered in water spots, those nasty little polka dots in your paint that look like they're just under the surface and won't come out no matter hard you scrub. This is probably not where the expression "spit and polish" comes from, but go ahead and spit on your car. Remember when your mom would spit onto a hanky to scrub your face? Well, it works for the water spots on your car, too. Spit right onto the water spots and give them a rub with your finger. The water spots should come right out. You can also rub them off with a damp chamois.

Once your car's clean, you might want to take a few minutes to lubricate all your locks and hinges to keep them working smoothly and to avoid corrosion. But make sure you're using

> ### Lisa's Tip
> Your car may come with a tiny can of touch-up paint. Use it if you notice any nicks or chips in your paint. If water gets between your paint and the car's metal frame, rust will form. If you don't have any touch-up paint on hand, or if it's not the right color, a dab of clear nail polish will do the trick.

the right stuff; pick up some lock lube for the door locks, and the stuff in a spray can for the hinges. If you're not sure, ask the clerk at the local auto supply shop or hardware store.

Tire Pressure

Good tires keep you on the road, and you know by now how important proper tire maintenance is for safety. It's a good idea for you to know how to take care of your own tires, how to change them in a pinch and, of course, how to fill them up with air.

Let's start with a tire gauge. Every car ought to have one. Pick up a good one and toss it into the glove box. Find the tire placard on your car. This is a little placard that tells you all you need to know about your tires and what tire pressure is recommended for your car. The placard may be on the inside of a door pillar or in the glove box. Your owner's manual should tell you where to find it. Read the placard carefully because the front and back tires might have different recommended pressures. (You can also check the tires themselves. See Chapter 3 for details.)

Once you know how much air to put into your tires, pop on over to your local service station and fill the tires with air. Remove the tire valve cap, and make sure you've got it in a safe place. I mentioned in Chapter 3 how important that little doo-dad is for keeping dirt and moisture out of the valve, so make sure you don't lose it. Press the tire gauge down firmly onto the valve, being sure that you've got a good seal. As you press down you might hear a short burst of air, and that's okay. Anything more, though, means that your seal isn't tight enough and you're letting air out of your tire. So press it down on the valve just long enough for the indicator to extend from the bottom of the gauge. Compare the reading on the gauge to the tire placard. If you need more air, go ahead and fill the tire. Then check it again. If you put in too much, let a little out by pushing down on the pin inside the tire valve. For best results, do this when your tires are cold.

Once you're satisfied that you've got the right amount of air in each tire, replace the valve cap, and off you go.

There, don't you feel like a seasoned mechanic? Now that you're comfortable doing a bit of work on your own car, you'll be able to save yourself a trip to the garage and some money as well. But don't tell your mechanic; the last thing I need is for my colleagues to think I've been giving away trade secrets.

7

Preventing and Dealing with Emergencies

An ounce of prevention is worth a pound of cure, right? That's the idea behind preventive medicine. Isn't it better to avoid getting sick? So far we've been talking about the regular upkeep and maintenance of your car, which is exactly that ounce of prevention a driver needs. Accidents happen, though. And little problems do pop up even if you've been really good about taking care of your car. So in this chapter we'll talk about all the stuff you need to do to prevent problems and accidents, but we'll also discuss how to deal with these when they do come up.

You Can Tune a Piano, But Can You Tune a Car?

As you know from Chapter 2 mechanics no longer use the term "tune-up." Now we call them seasonal checkups because of how cars are built today. They used to come with all kinds of parts that needed to be changed regularly at one time or another. But with updates in technology, that's no longer the case. Many parts are made to last and need to be checked only once in a while to make sure they're still in good working order. So your seasonal checkup might come down to a simple scan test, like a diagnostic exam just to make sure that everything is okay. Of course, cars also come with a lot of electronics, and you've still got brakes, oil and fluids, all of which need to be serviced. Your tires still need to be rotated as well. So sometimes a checkup will involve an oil change and an inspection—a check of all belts, hoses, fluid levels and lights—and maybe a tire rotation.

The idea behind a regular checkup is to catch anything that might need servicing or fixing now, in order to prevent more expensive problems later. Why pay through the nose for something that a little preventive maintenance could have fixed? A regular seasonal checkup will likely cost you about an hour of labor, plus the oil change and the added cost of any needed repairs. But if you keep up a regular maintenance schedule, with regular seasonal checkups, chances are your mechanic won't find any major problems.

Not all seasonal checkups will require you to change your oil, by the way. However, you might be due for an oil change *between* regular checkups; oil changes are dictated by mileage, but remember that your mechanic might take the time, while changing your oil, to give your car the once-over, too.

Frankie Valli, Antonio Vivaldi, Your Car and You: The Four Seasons

As I said, mechanics talk in terms of seasonal checkups, with specific things to be taken care of at specific points in the year. Here is a breakdown of what you can expect to have done with each seasonal checkup.

Fall/Winter

Even though oil changes are dictated by mileage, your fall/winter checkup will probably include an oil change. The mechanic will also check your brakes, for obvious reasons, and she'll make sure the battery and electrical systems are in good working order. This is especially important in frigid climes. You'll need to be able to start your car on those really cold winter mornings, so you should make sure that your electrical system is in good shape. You should also have the antifreeze tested for strength. Antifreeze tends to break down over time, thus reducing its strength and its ability to keep things at an even temperature. Your mechanic will let you know if it needs to be changed.

You'll want to take the time to put on your winter tires. Remember that all-season tires are not good enough. And you should change all four, not just the two you think are important. So invest in a good, complete set of winter tires. You'll also want to replace the summer wiper blades with special winter blades that have a rubber covering to stop the wiper joint from freezing. And you shouldn't forget to change your windshield washer fluid: get rid of the pink bug juice that you've been using for the summer months and toss in the stuff that'll hold up to freezing temperatures.

> **Lisa's Tip**
> If you think your tire might be leaking, fill spay bottle with soapy water. Spray the tire, one side at a time, and look for bubbles. If they appear, you've found your hole.

While we're on the subject, please don't use water in the windshield washer reservoir. Many people think water is all you need in the summertime. But water doesn't clear your windshield. Think about it: the reason you have wipers in the first place is to get water off your windshield so that you can see. Furthermore, any water left over will freeze in the winter, blocking the flow of the windshield washer. You might be tempted to try to fix the problem by sticking a pin into the tiny holes where the washer solution sprays out, but this only ruins them, bending the conduits so that the liquid squirts every which way except onto your windshield. Simple rule: your windshield washer reservoir is for windshield washer solution, the pink or yellow stuff in the summer, and the blue or green stuff in the winter.

Now your car is ready for winter driving. Are you? Be safe on the roads. Just because you've got the best snow tires around doesn't mean you can drive like a cowboy; others on the road might not be as confident as you, and if you're speeding (which you shouldn't do anyway), you'll make them nervous and probably spray slush and snow onto their windshields, affecting their visibility. Remember that you can cause an accident without being in one. Be considerate, slow down and remember to keep a safe distance between you and the car in front.

Checklist Seasonal Checkup Checklist

Do you change things around in your coat closet when the seasons change? Maybe move those spring jackets to the basement and dig out your boots, gloves, hat and scarf? Your car needs the same kind of attention. Consult the following checklist in the spring and again in the fall:

✔ Switch wiper blades.
✔ Change windshield washer fluid.
✔ Change tires.
✔ Change oil.
✔ Clean out trunk.
✔ Check spare tire and jack.
✔ Perform walk-around inspection (look for loose moldings and hoses, paint chips, scratches, etc.).

Springtime

Once you and your car are through the ravages of winter, you'll find a whole new set of challenges to face in the spring, such as potholes, which pop up like perennials. Your car has already suffered enough abuse through the winter. You know what I'm talking about, those times when you were stuck on the ice, or stuck in a snowbank, and rather than shovel your way out you gunned the engine and smoked the tires to get unstuck. At times your engine may have been revving up at around 3,000 RPMs. That's really hard on the transmission and the engine, as well as on the front end. The spring checkup will show you just how badly you've hurt your car.

First, you'll want to have the air filter checked. A car picks up a lot of moisture and sludge and dirt throughout the winter, so you'll want to make sure the air filter is not all gunked up. Again, you may or may not be due for an oil change, depending on the mileage. You'll also need to have the winter tires removed as soon as is safely possible. A lot of lazy car owners drive on their winter tires well into the spring. If this is you, start saving up for another set. The rising springtime temperatures will adversely affect the tires. They'll break down in the heat much more quickly than they would when used for their correct application in the cold and the snow. Prolonged contact with dry roads is also not good for winter tires. So, as soon as is safe, switch 'em for the summer set.

You should check the brakes next. If you've managed to survive pothole season, and after you get your summer tires put on, check the front end, the suspension and the alignment, because you'll want to make sure the car drives straight after all the stuff you've bumped into or slid on during the winter. Last, but certainly not least, you should put your summer wiper blades back on and store the winter ones for next year.

Summertime

With the kids in your neighborhood playing outside and yours shuttling off to day camp or soccer practice, you'll want to make sure the car is safe because you'll be carrying precious cargo. You'll want to make sure the car handles well and brakes well; you never know when a stray bouncing ball will be followed by a small child darting out from between two parked cars. When that happens you'll want that car to stop on a dime. The way I see it, it's more important for kids to run around without worrying about being hit by a car than it is for someone to go from 0 to 60 before reaching the end of the block, especially if they haven't had their brakes checked yet!

Now would also be a good time to check the cooling and air conditioning systems, not because there is necessarily anything wrong with them, but to make sure that nothing will go wrong, especially if you're planning to go on a long road trip. All of this costs money, I know. But we are creatures of comfort: we like the car to get us to work on time, but we also like the radio, CD player and air conditioner to function.

If you're thinking of taking a road trip, you'll want to make sure the car is in good shape, so take care of those little things that you might have left out in the spring checkup. You'll want your vacation to be stress-free all the way from here to wherever you're off to. You don't want to have a problem pop up along the way, especially one that could have been prevented with a simple checkup.

Tuning up your air conditioner

This is not a do-it-yourself job. Because of the equipment and the environmental issue of recuperating (or verifying) the gases, which involves sophisticated machinery and expertise that the average driver does not have, there are only a few things you can do yourself on the air conditioner. In many parts of North America, you have to be a certified air conditioning technician to do this job. But even if this is not true where you live, you don't want to mess with this stuff; have a professional take care of it for you.

One thing you *can* do yourself is flush out the air conditioner's condenser. Break out the garden hose. You see, air has to circulate to let the air conditioner work properly. If your condenser (a kind of radiator) is gunked up with dirt, bugs, etc., then air won't flow, and the system will overheat. So grab the hose, pop open the hood and spray water at the car's radiator. The condenser is right behind it, so you'll be rinsing off your radiator at the same time. (Do I have to remind you to make sure that your engine is cold?)

Finally, you should have an air conditioning performance test done by a professional. This basically involves checking the pressure of the gases that make the air conditioner work. It's a good idea to have the system checked once a year rather than wait until you have a problem. Again, preventive maintenance is the key.

> **Lisa's Tip**
> You should run your air conditioner, even in the winter. Just a few minutes of use will prevent the seals from drying out, and it's a great way to de-mist your windows on a winter morning.

On the Road: Preparing for a Long Road Trip

You've been planning a road trip for a long time—a camping trip or a junket to see Grandma and Grandpa. You want your trip to go off without a hitch (unless, of course, you're pulling a trailer, in which case you'll need a hitch, but I digress). You don't want to have to stop in the middle of nowhere and walk to the first little grease-covered garage you find, where an unseasoned mechanic might charge you who knows how much for who knows what. So take care of your car well before you plan to leave. *Never have a major repair done a week before your road trip*. Why? Because new parts can break down, so you want to give your car a good month to drive around on any new parts you've had to install. That way any kinks can be taken care of before your vacation.

Once everything checks out mechanically, your work begins. How can you prepare for that long road trip? Empty the car out completely: go through the glove box, your cubbyholes and your ashtray if you're a nonsmoker, because that's where you hide all your junk, right? Check between and underneath the seats. Check the trunk. Why are you doing this? You need everything out of the car so that you can be sure that you have your road map, that you've checked the expiry date on the first-aid kit, that you have the spare tire, and that your jack is working properly. You may even want to have the spare checked again, because there's nothing like having a flat tire and then jacking up your car on the side of the highway only to find that your spare is flat, too.

Before you leave, make sure you know where you're going and how to get back. Have a couple of maps handy. If you're a member of AAA or CAA you can order a TripTik, a foldout map with directions and other information to make your trip easy and enjoyable. Make sure your membership is up to date! If you have a few maps, you can highlight specific things on each; for example, you can highlight restaurants on one map, sightseeing spots on another, etc. And don't forget to pick up some travel insurance.

Preparing for Emergencies: What to Pack

I'm the only person I know who can get stranded in the woods for three days and come out having gained weight. But that's only because I come prepared, and then some. The size of your survival kit will depend on the size of your car and where you're driving. If you're staying in the city you'll just need the basics, but if you're going on a road trip then you're going to have to pack some amenities. I've got a three-day pack in the trunk of my car with a compact thermal sleeping bag and an emergency shelter (a little pup tent you string between two trees to keep the rain off you. It's bright orange so that I can be seen if I'm lost). I've got canned heat (no, not the blues band from the '60s, but the combustible stuff in a tin). If you don't have canned heat, a candle can save your life. Just make sure you use the candle correctly (don't drip wax on the dash, stick the lit candle there and fall asleep). And I've got something from a company called Hot Pack Enterprises®, which makes meals that heat themselves. I also have a bottle of water, beef jerky and candy (not chocolate, though, because that can get messy in the summertime).

You'll also need a flashlight with spare batteries. And you should have some rope and matches. Keep the matches in a plastic bag to keep them dry. If you take medication, make sure you've got a three- to five-day supply with you in the car at all times. You might also want to bring a Swiss Army knife, or a reasonable facsimile, along with a cell phone. Wrap your first-aid kit in something soft, and have it in the car, not the trunk. Put it underneath the seat so that it won't fly around inside the car in an accident. You'd feel pretty silly if you got beaned in the head by a first-aid kit!

With current advances in technology, we're seeing a lot more cars with **global positioning systems (GPS)**, like GM's "On Star" and other variations. These systems will virtually eliminate the need for my style of survival kit. They make it possible for a company to unlock your car by remote control if you ever lock your keys inside. Or if your "check engine" light comes on, a service agent can talk to you directly to help you figure out what's wrong. If you're ever in an accident and can't move or speak, these types of systems monitor your car's emergency systems and can send emergency crews your way. It's amazing, to say the least, but also costly.

How to survive being stranded in your car

If you're a fan of *Survivor*, you probably watch the show thinking "I could do that…for a million bucks." Granted, being stranded in your car at the side of a highway in the middle of nowhere isn't nearly as glamorous as, say, the Australian Outback or the Amazon. Still, let me give you some basic survival techniques. I'm afraid you'll have to make your own fortune, though.

Just as there are seasonal checkups for your car, so there are seasonal survival techniques. You might find yourself stranded in a raging winter storm or caught with a flat in the middle of nowhere. Let's get you prepared for such scenarios.

Panic kills. In a worst-case scenario, if you're stranded in the middle of nowhere, with no cell phone, no way of getting in touch with anyone, and you're trapped, you could die. It comes down to attitude; cool heads really do prevail. If you come to the conclusion that you're going to be spending the night in your car, possibly hurt, make the conscious decision that you're going to make it. Scientists believe that a good, positive outlook on life can prevent a cold. It could also keep you alive in a dangerous situation. Focus on what's important to you; think about the reasons you need to survive.

You need shelter, heat, food and liquid. Without shelter you're exposed to the elements and leave yourself open to hypothermia or sunstroke. You should have candles or canned heat, an emergency blanket and all of the other stuff we've talked about. If you can make it through one night, chances are you will survive. If you don't use a cell phone in your everyday life, you might want to invest in an emergency phone with a calling card. Keep in mind, though, that it might not work in all situations, for example, if you're out of the signal range or if your battery's dead.

Keep your mind focused. Write things down if you're able to. Do you know where you are? Do you know what day it is? What happened? Writing it down helps you to keep focused, and obviously the information will help emergency crews.

You don't have to remember all of this; just keep this book in your glove box for quick reference.

The ol' spare tire

Don't let the above section scare you; few of us ever find ourselves in such life-and-death situations. It is far more likely that one of your tires will blow while you're driving on the highway some day. Rather than wait around for a tow truck, you may as well go ahead and change the tire by yourself, and then drive to the nearest garage to have your blown tire fixed. Changing a flat tire is one of the easiest and most basic do-it-yourself jobs. In fact, you should have been told how to do this when you took drivers' education classes. But if you don't know how, here's a crash course.

First things first: find out where the heck your spare tire is. All it takes is a quick glance in the owner's manual. Some larger cars come equipped with a full-sized spare. If you've got an SUV or a similar-sized vehicle, the spare tire is stored on the back against the door, or sometimes even attached to your car's underbody. Smaller cars usually come with a space-saver spare. It's a smaller wheel meant to be used just to get you to a garage. Manufacturers sometimes store it in the oddest of places, which is why you need to consult the owner's manual. Your car probably also comes with a simple jack, *intended only for changing a tire, and not for getting underneath the car*. It's quite simple to use. Take a few minutes to learn how it works.

Now that you know where the spare is, here's how to change it. Eventually you're going to have to jack up the car, but that's not your first step. What you want to do first is loosen the bolts that hold your wheel on. They're usually on pretty tight, so they'll require physical effort just to loosen them. If you're doing that while the car is up on a jack, you could push the car off the jack and risk injury. So, using the tire iron that comes with your car, loosen the bolts.

Go ahead and jack up the car just enough to get the tire off and get the spare on. Remove the already loosened bolts with your fingers, and watch where you put them because you'll need them. If you've had to remove a hub cap, for example, place it face down on the ground and put the bolts inside it for safe keeping. Pull off the flat tire and replace it with the spare.

Now you simply work backward. Replace the bolts, finger-tight only, for now. Let the car down off the jack, then tighten the bolts with the tire iron. Put the flat tire in the trunk or hatchback, and put away your jack and tire iron. You're done. Good job!

Remember, your spare tire is intended to get you to a garage, not to drive on for long stretches. So if you're on a highway and you've just changed your tire, get off as soon as you can and find a garage.

3

The Car Owner and the Environment

It's de rigueur to be environmental these days. We all bring our recycling boxes to the curb, packed with empty cans and old newspapers. Some of us even have a compost heap in our garden, and we all feel very good about doing our part. But how many car owners and drivers really think about the impact that their cars and their driving habits have on the environment? Pollution, global warming and the greenhouse effect are major concerns for everyone, but environmental experts tell us that it's drivers who are causing all the problems, as we let our cars spew exhaust, burn oil and idle for longer than necessary.

Well, everything we've talked about up to this point, whether it's tire maintenance or changing the oil, has an effect on our environment. Consider this: every 10 days motorists who drive with underinflated tires and poorly maintained engines waste 70 million gallons (265 million liters) of gasoline. There are other statistics that are just as staggering, and I'll tell you about them as we go along. You see, you don't have to be a New Age, latter-day hippie to care about the environment. You just need a little information to give you the impetus to maintain your car properly. And that's really all it takes. You've heard about so-called clean gasoline, or clean-burning fuel.

That's a start. But regular checkups and oil changes, maintaining your tire pressure, even watching your speed, can all help make you a more environmentally friendly car owner, and I hope to make you a more environmentally conscious driver as well. So whether you're into Birkenstocks or construction boots, dashikis or coveralls, patchouli oil or motor oil, in this chapter you'll learn how you can do your part to protect the environment.

All Revved Up and No Place to Go

Let's start with a simple request. If you're waiting for someone in your car and you know you've got a bit of a wait ahead of you, please turn off your engine. There is no reason to let your car run, spewing wasted exhaust into the air we all have to breathe. If your car isn't maintained properly (which shouldn't be the case if you've read this far), your exhaust can be particularly damaging. Consider that in some cities it is actually illegal to let your car idle for longer than four minutes, punishable by fines. There is no reason this kind of thinking

West Nile Virus? In a Book about Auto Mechanics?

Tire fires seem to burn forever. The thick black smoke that billows from mounds of improperly disposed-of tires that have been set aflame is poison, plain and simple, and wreaks havoc with the environment. Tire fires have also been known to be a breeding ground for mosquitoes, which, in these days of the West Nile virus, should be a sufficient incentive for you to dispose of your old tires properly. Talk to your mechanic or contact your community's waste management or environment authority for information about where to take your old tires.

can't be extended to every community and every car-owning household.

You might also be the sort of driver who warms up the car on cold winter mornings, letting the engine idle for up to five minutes. That's no longer necessary. Today's cars are designed to warm up so quickly that you don't have to let them idle in the winter.

Waste Not, Want Not

"Reuse" is one of the cardinal tenets of an environmentally conscious society, one that applies just as much to tires as to anything else. Some car companies are looking into ways to reuse old car parts and are sending less and less material to the landfill. Indeed, these days old rubber tires are finding their way into the most surprising places. It's kind of like reincarnation, really. You might remember playing on a backyard swing made from an old tractor tire when you were a child. These days several types of playground toys are made from old tires that have been broken down into what's called "rubber crumb," left over from tires that have been stripped down. In the recycling process, all of a tire's parts—the fibers, the steel and of course the rubber—are separated and reused. There are even companies out there that turn old tires into fashion, making very stylish purses and sandals. They are said to be virtually indestructible and are purported to never go out of style. Tires have also been used to resurface roads. And one car company is looking into ways to use old tires in the manufacture of their owner's manuals. They hope to publish the pages in a rubber binder made from old tires.

Taking the Pressure Off

We've talked about the importance of maintaining proper tire pressure. Now that you know how to "read" tires and how to maintain them properly, you have no excuse not to do so. Consider how much fuel you waste when your tires are improperly inflated. Remember the statistic I quoted at the beginning of the chapter? Underinflation wastes fuel because the flab, for lack of a better term, causes drag, slowing your car. Then your engine has to use more power to keep the car rolling, which means you're hitting the gas pedal harder, using more gas, causing more exhaust. A similar problem occurs when your wheels are unaligned. Your car has to work harder not only to keep itself straight, but also to keep rolling. In this case, too, the driver has to compensate for resistance with more pressure on the gas pedal.

Need a financial incentive? If you don't maintain your tires properly, they won't last as long, and you'll have to replace them more often. In many countries, not only will you pay the cost of new tires, you'll also pay an environmental levy. That's what you're charged each time you purchase new tires, presumably to compensate for the cost of getting rid of them. From a purely environmental point of view, the more often you purchase tires, the more tires will be sent to the landfill. So, you see, proper tire maintenance is good on so many levels, saving you money, saving you gas and saving your future.

Never Mind the Air Conditioning, Environmental Thinking Is Cool Enough

Most air conditioning systems these days are easier on the environment than ever before. People used to think that using the air conditioner wasted gas. There was a time when the physical weight of the old AC systems was significant, causing drag. Today's newer materials are much lighter. You now have more air drag and waste more gas if you have your windows rolled down and your sunroof open. You might feel cooler with the wind in your hair, but with all these openings compromising your car's aerodynamics, you're slowing the car down and using more gas to keep your speed up. Not everyone likes air conditioning, though. Some prefer to drive with the windows open. I don't suppose there is really anything wrong with that, as long as you are aware of the effect that has on your wallet and on the environment.

If you do have an AC system in your car, again, like anything else, proper maintenance is key. As I mentioned in the last chapter, you should have it serviced only by a technician certified and competent to handle and recycle the refrigerants. Many older air conditioners contain those pesky CFCs that have been implicated in the depletion of the ozone layer. According to the Environmental Protection Agency, almost one-third of the CFCs released into the atmosphere come from mobile air conditioning units.

Liquid Refreshment

How important is it to recycle or to properly dispose of used fluids? Consider this statistic from the Automotive Information Council. Remember the *Exxon Valdez*? Well, every year almost 20 times the amount of oil spilled by the doomed tanker gets dumped into the environment by uninformed do-it-yourselfers. Thanks to this book you won't be one of those.

Any time you're dealing with fluids that might pose a danger, find out how to dispose of them properly. When you try to hide old oil or dump it in the sewer, justifying it by saying, "Oh well, it's only a little, nobody will know," imagine what happens when so many others think that way. The same goes for all fluids, including old antifreeze and even old car batteries. Many service centers accept waste oil, antifreeze and old tires. Ask your mechanic or contact your community's environmental authority or waste management people about where to go.

Speed Limits

There is a reason for speed limits that goes beyond simply slowing you down. Believe me, the authorities aren't trying to hinder your freedom or to make extra money off speedsters. Did you know that your gas mileage actually goes down when you drive above the posted speed limit? When you cruise at 55 mph or 90 km/h, for example, your engine is at optimum efficiency. When you start going over the speed limit, you're forcing your engine and consuming more fuel, therefore creating more exhaust. The trick to fuel economy is to keep your speed as steady as possible. Avoid sudden acceleration and use cruise control on the open highways to keep your speed as even as possible. As a bonus, you'll find that on those long road trips cruise control will leave you feeling less tired.

Know Your Limits

The history of speed limits in the United States is interesting, to say the least. Up until 1972, individual states were allowed to set their own maximum speed limits, and most pegged it at 70 mph (115 km/h). When the energy crisis hit, however, the government was desperate to curb the country's massive fuel consumption. It linked a 55 mph (90 km/h) speed limit with continued funding for state highway programs, effectively ensuring state cooperation. Shortly after, the Transportation Research Board announced that the reduced speed had saved more than 9,000 lives. Despite the good news, some states argued for a higher upper limit. After much debate, control was returned to the states. Today, maximum speed limits vary from state to state, although most remain at 55 mph (90 km/h).

You also want to keep those extra pounds off; less weight means better mileage. Unload your trunk whenever possible, and try not to have too much stuff in a roof rack. Carpool whenever you can. Consider the old park-and-ride. And you might want to think about consolidating your errands, mapping out your Saturday trips to the store and the market so that you waste less fuel.

Environmentally Friendly Cars

Environmentally friendly cars, hybrid cars, electric cars, hydrogen cars and fuel cells are all very trendy ideas right now. You might actually see some of these on the road, but there aren't many of them. At least not yet. But every year the technology gets better and better and the car manufacturers get closer to building reliable, cost-efficient hybrid cars.

If you drive long distances a hybrid car might be right up your alley for fuel economy and ecology. We just don't know how much repairs will cost yet, because the technology is so new that there are a limited number of mechanics who service these vehicles. Right now hybrids are more of a novelty and their prices and repair costs can be prohibitive. We need more of these vehicles to be produced, though, so that more of them are on the road. As the technology becomes mainstream, the kinks will be worked out and the environment will benefit.

9

How to Buy and Sell a Car

Having read through eight chapters of this thing, you now know all you need to know about owning a car. But do you even *have* a car? If you haven't got the requisite set of wheels, then all of this has been purely academic. So let's get you a car.

There are some things you'll need to know when buying a car. First, you need to decide what kind of car you want, what kind of car is best for you. There are few things more exciting than buying a new car. But as a consumer, you need to know how to protect yourself against a raw deal, whether you're buying a brand-new car or a used (or "pre-owned") one. By the same token, there is also a right way to *sell* a car, although, as we'll see a bit further on, the essential thing is to be up front and honest whether buying or selling.

A Man's Car Is His Castle

Some people, for one reason or another, live in their cars. I'll explain: I don't mean to be insensitive to the homeless, nor am I suggesting you sell your house and move into your car to save on mortgage payments. I just want you to be in the right mindset when you decide to invest in a new car, because buying a car is probably your second-largest expense after buying a house.

When it comes to a house, everyone talks about the resale value: buy a house now, then double your money when you sell it later. But unlike a house, a car *loses* value, and is usually worth a lot less down the road, as it were. In fact, a new car loses value immediately after purchase. They say that your car's value goes down even as you drive it off the lot. In that sense a new car is always a losing investment. So spend wisely.

Buying a New Car

Deciding whether to buy a new car or a secondhand car isn't always a question of price. For many people it comes down to safety or fashion. There's no real mystery there; it simply depends on what you want. Something sensible and economical? A family van? A sports coupe? Does it match your handbag?

It's also a question of how much car you really need. Does it need to be big and tough, like Arnold Schwarzenegger's Hummer? Does it need to do 0 to 60 in under a minute? Those are purely personal decisions. The truth is that not a lot of people need a big 4x4 these days, and nobody needs a sedan that rivals a Formula 1 car for speed. Most of us just want something that'll get us from point A to point B safely and economically.

Footwork

Being a responsible and diligent consumer takes footwork. Once you decide what kind of car you want, you will need to do some research. These days, it's no longer common to see someone drive around in what we used to call a boat—a large, unwieldy car like a big old Cadillac or a Lincoln Continental. Cars are generally made smaller. Have a look at the parking spaces on a downtown main street. Does it seem like there is room for at least two Mini Coopers in one space? That's because parking spaces are still measured and drawn with dimensions appropriate for bigger cars. Most people, however, find a compact car more than adequate for city driving. Compacts are small and practical, and newer ones have a lot more space inside than they used to. You can easily pick up a good 4-cylinder car with power options and luxury items such as leather seats and a sunroof; it'll also have the bonus of good fuel economy and high resale value. Just to be clear, by high resale value I don't mean you'll make a profit on your original investment like you would for a house. But you might find you can sell your car for more than you would have otherwise imagined.

A minivan may be more your style, even though it's not the most economical or environmental vehicle. But it is the best type of car to buy in terms of value, since minivans come with lots of stuff at low cost.

The ads

You should always approach new-car ads with a grain of salt. Car advertising is designed simply to get you into the showroom, and the ads are designed with different types of consumers in mind. For example, some dealers will promote excitement, which comes down to speed and adventure. If you're the sporty, outdoorsy type, then you might be attracted by an ad for a truck that can climb Mount Kilimanjaro. Other companies might simply promote the value of their cars by advertising the ever-popular zero-percent financing, attractive to those on a budget—and who isn't these days?

There is also a rational or practical side to car ads, which is why so many commercials or magazine ads feature children and families.

Sex is still used in car advertising, but not as much as before. Car companies have come to realize that sex isn't what's most important to potential buyers. On the other hand, some car dealers have been turning to celebrities such as Diana Krall to sell their cars. These companies are basing their strategy on marketing and demographics: their research tells them that their ideal clients are listening to these stars' music. Car manufacturers will dangle whatever carrots they think will get customers into their showrooms.

Ultimately, though, it comes down to what *you* want, rather than what the advertiser wants to sell you. The more you know about what you want, the less susceptible you'll be to advertising or marketing gimmicks. Know thyself, Socrates once famously said. And while I'm sure he wasn't thinking of new-car purchases at the time, it's still damned good advice.

Leasing and financing: A tongue twister

Not very many of us have the cash on hand to buy a car outright. Typically, new-car buyers will finance the car over time, or even lease it with the option to buy. But as I'll explain further on, the disadvantages of leasing outweigh the advantages for most drivers. Some businesses will lease a car because it makes more economic sense. They can usually exchange the car after a certain period and, assuming it was driven under normal conditions, not be held responsible for a reasonable amount of wear and tear.

If you plan to lease a car, try to get the lowest monthly payment with no money down. If your car is lost or written off, you will lose whatever money you did put down. Some people make the mistake of leasing specifically because they don't have the cash to plonk down on a new car. But if you factor in the interest on your monthly payments, the money you'll have to put down if you plan to purchase the car you've been leasing, and the interest on the loan you'll likely need in order to make that final payment, you'll see that you're probably paying thousands more than if you'd just gone ahead and bought the car in the beginning. Generally, the Automobile Protection Association (APA) will tell you that if you can't afford to buy a new car, you can't afford to lease one. You're probably better off looking for a good used car.

If you do purchase a new car, make sure you ask about financing. Keep in mind, though, that if you finance through a bank that the dealer recommends, the dealer is more often than not getting a kickback. That means that the bank gives back the dealer some of the money it makes off the deal. So it's best, whenever possible, to finance directly through the dealer.

Chances are you'll get a better price for the car and a better financing deal. Try to get the lowest possible "all-in-one" price for the car you're buying, meaning one with everything (taxes, freight, warranty, etc.) included.

Let's make a deal

As I mentioned above, it takes work to make sure you're getting the best deal. Getting a good deal is easy when you're buying groceries. You check the flyers, you clip coupons and you buy certain products in places that give you better deals. It gets a little more complicated when you're buying a car, but the principle is the same. When you head down to the dealer, bring an ad with you. Ads can often be misleading, but you may not realize it until you actually see the car in question and get the opportunity to talk with the salesperson.

Keep in mind that whomever you end up dealing with wants to make a sale. It might be a good idea to bring along a competitor's ad as well. If you've got the savvy and the intestinal fortitude, you might get the salesperson to match the competitor's price. But don't stop there. It might take a bit o' back and forth, but if he is indeed willing to match the competitor's price, then go to the competitor to see if she'll go even lower. Eventually you'll find a car and a price you're comfortable with, and you'll be ready to spend the dough.

A competent salesperson should be able to talk knowledgeably about the car you're thinking of buying. That means he should be able to discuss all aspects of the car with you, including the recommended features. He should be willing and able to respond to all of your concerns, and he should offer you a road test. Since buying a car is such a huge expense, this whole song and dance is bound to be a stressful experience. Thankfully, there are consumer protection organizations that have your best interests at heart. In the United States, there's the National Highway Traffic Safety Administration. In Canada, there's the Automobile Protection Association. Organizations like these, or others such as the Better Business Bureaus, can point you in the right direction and help you arm yourself for when you have to face the dealership.

Proper timing can also help you get a good deal. The best

time to buy a car is just before Christmas, when dealers are sure to offer you the best rebates. So watch for the ads and for the specials, and don't be afraid to take advantage of them.

It's also a good idea to have your old car appraised just in case you want to use it on a trade-in. Chances are, though, that your new dealer won't be interested in your old car, especially if it's a North American model. The used-car market is saturated right now, and your car's value might not be deemed worth the trade. Keep that in mind when you're shopping around.

I'll Buy Your Car on One Condition...: Buying Used

When you buy a used car, you're picking up all that it's been through with its previous owner—its bumps, bruises, wears and tears. Therefore, the car's condition should be your main focus. The biggest mistake people make when they're shopping around for a used car is believing what they're told by the seller. It's an old cliché, but if it sounds or looks too good to be true, it probably is. This is especially important when you're buying a car advertised in the classified section of your local newspaper. If you call someone and he asks you something like, "Which car are you calling about?" it means that he's selling more than one car. And that probably means that he's a professional salesman working on the side, what we call a "curb-sider" (a professional who is not registered). If you're not sure who you're dealing with, and if you suspect that the guy on the phone is a dealer, ask to see the records, licensing, insurance and any other papers that go with the car. Ask for the service records. If he can't produce this material, he obviously doesn't know much about the car. That's a sign that you should probably walk away. If you're brave and crafty and you're still interested in buying the car, try to bargain him down.

If you find a car that you think might be worth buying, then have it checked out (see sidebar on page 129). You should also make sure the car you are about to buy is free from liens. A lien is a debt still owed on the car by the current owner to a financing company. Think of it like buying a house and taking over the previous owner's mortgage. That's a burden you don't want. In the United States, CarFax provides vehicle history reports for a reasonable fee (see Resources). In Canada, check a provincial registry, or call the APA and ask them to do a lien search. This is something you won't have to worry about if you buy from a dealer.

Checklist Used Vehicle Inspection Checklist

In addition to making sure that the obvious things work (wipers, clock, radio, heater, air conditioning, lights, etc.), there are a few other areas you can check out yourself:

- ✔ Paint (Check around tailpipe and windows for over-spray, which could indicate that the car has been repainted.)
- ✔ Body (Do "ripples" appear anywhere on the body? Are panels misaligned?)
- ✔ Leaks (Check under the vehicle for fluid spots.)
- ✔ Tires (Check the treads for uneven wear, which could indicate the need for an alignment.)
- ✔ Rust (Check the entire car.)
- ✔ Shocks (Good shocks shouldn't bounce more than twice.)
- ✔ Interior (Pull back carpets and look for signs of leaks or rust.)
- ✔ Oil level (If it's low, it may be an indication that the car burns oil.)
- ✔ Exhaust (Blue or black smoke indicates a problem.)

If you're inclined to do the work, you can check out a used car's history to find out if it's been in any accidents or if the owner is being up front with you about maintenance and repairs. You can do that by taking the car to a dealer. If you're able to determine the dealer who originally sold the car—some use stickers on special license plate covers—start there. The service department should have a computerized record of the car's service history. If you don't know where the car was purchased, try taking it to your regular mechanic for a once-over. Obvious body work or new parts can hint at the type of work that may have been done. You can also research a used car's ownership history by going through the proper authorities. In the United States, CarFax can provide this service. In Canada, CarProof provides the same service (see Resources).

Most people, however, don't go that far. The car's service and ownership history aren't as important as having the car checked. A good mechanic ought to be able to tell you things about the car that the owner might not have wanted you to know. She should be able to tell you, for example, if the mileage has been tampered with. By the way, don't put too much faith in a road test. Use it purely as a tactic: if the seller won't let you take the car off the property, don't buy the car. But even if you do take a used car on a road test, how are you going to know if it's any good? Try renting a similar one. Drive it around for a while and compare the used car in question with the rented one.

Hey, this car has no steering wheel!

Congratulations on your new purchase. Now, what do you do if your new but very used car starts to give you trouble after the cash has changed hands? Did you make sure to protect yourself with a sales contract? "Buyer beware" is really the best advice when it comes to these types of transactions, but some laws do exist to protect you. For instance, some states and provinces have labeling requirements on used cars that demand openness on the part of the seller as to the car's previous use, any repairs that have been done, any repairs still needed, costs and so on. These are the rules, but they are rarely enforced. If they were, you wouldn't even have to have the car checked.

Lisa's Tip

Before buying a used car, look for rust in the following places: under the floor mats, under carpets, inside trunk wells, door panels and under the vehicle.

Selling Your Car

The sales contract is a good idea even if you're the one selling the car. The ideal situation when selling or buying is an open and honest deal in which both parties are up front about everything. If you're the one selling, you want to be honest about the car's history and condition. In other words, let a potential buyer know everything you'd want to know if you were the buyer. As long as the buyer is aware, then she won't have any grounds to sue you farther down the road.

You can't fool me; there's no sanity clause

A good way for both parties to protect themselves is to draft a proper sales contract. You could put together a homemade contract, or use the contract templates available from the APA.

You need the date, the car's price and serial number, the seller's and the buyer's information, and details as to the condition of the car. The current owner—that's you—would stipulate any warranties included in the sale and might include a special clause that would cancel any legal recourse the buyer would have after the sale. That means the buyer purchases your car at his own risk ("sold without any warranties against hidden defects"). That kind of statement protects you, the seller. However, some consumer protection agencies don't recommend it because it can be used in bad faith. That is to say, a dishonest seller (not you, of course) could sell the car with hidden defects and could include the clause just to save his backside.

There will need to be a bit of government involvement in the sale of any car. Make sure to check with state or provincial authorities before selling or buying. If the car is going to cross a border, you may need to meet certain requirements to ensure smooth sailing.

What's my car worth, and how much can I get for it?

We've all heard the urban myth about the woman who sold a fancy sports car for only $50. Her husband, it seems, had left for a younger woman and sent his wife a telegram saying, "Sell the car, and send me what you get for it."

How do you know how much your car is worth? Look at ads for similar cars and compare. Even good guidebooks are purely theoretical, at best, and can be a bit off in the estimation of a car's real worth. There are complex calculations that go into determining a car's worth. A good guide such as the *Kelley Blue Book* in the United States, or the Automobile Protection Association's *Complete Canadian Used Car Guide* in Canada can help you figure it out.

Dollars, taxes

You didn't think you'd get away without paying taxes, did you? Whether you're buying or selling in the United States or Canada, there will be taxes involved. The amount of sales tax payable differs from state to state and province to province. Be sure to check the laws and procedures of transferring a title in your area. Since the tax is generally based on the selling price, some people figure they can get away with paying less if the selling price is doctored down. Don't try this at home! The government is not stupid—well at least not when it comes to collecting taxes. Just like you, tax people can look up the *Blue Book* value of a car. If your make and model is generally worth $10,000 and your bill of sale says you bought it for $1,500, a red flag will go up somewhere. The repercussions—which could include a nasty letter, an investigation and possibly jail time—are probably more than you bargained for!

Conclusion: The Clued-In Mechanic

So here we are at the end of the book. You and I are ready to part ways, little Grasshopper. I hope I've given you, my budding car expert, the tools you'll need to be the responsible car owner I know you can be. If you've paid any attention at all, you now know that your car is as deserving of tender loving care as, say, a loyal pet. And like that pet, your car can and will thrive with the proper care. Remember to check its fluids, replace its filters, take it for regular tune-ups and even wash it once in a while and you'll likely be rewarded with a long in happy relationship.

That's all I have to tell you. You're on your own now. But remember, like Glinda the Car Witch of the North, or ET: The Engine Terrestrial, I'll always be nearby—at least as long as you remember to keep this little book in your glove box next to your car owner's manual. Happy trails!

Glossary of Terms: Carspeak

Conversing intelligently about your car can require knowledge of a whole new language: carspeak. Here's a quick rundown of the terminology you'll need to sound a little less clueless:

air dams: Air dams are devices made of metal or plastic. Car manufacturers fit them beneath the front bumper of a car to block the flow of turbulent air under the chassis and improve aerodynamics and stability.

air filter: A nifty device made of paper and fiber that cleans the air of impurities as it enters the engine's cylinder for the combustion process. The end result? A smoother-running engine.

alternator: The alternator is part of your car's electrical system—the network that carries power to your headlights, fans, ignition coils, radio, air conditioning, etc. Lots of people think that power comes from the battery, but the real source for all of that energy is the gas tank. And the link from the gas tank to the battery is the alternator. It's a cool little device that converts power from the gasoline engine that drives you along the road, to electrical energy that keeps your battery working.

antilock brake system (ABS): This computer-controlled system prevents your brakes from locking or jamming. While this does reduce the risk of skids or slides, it does not erase the need to drive carefully or leave enough room for stopping.

ball joint: Now stop snickering! The ball joint is a ball-and-socket contraption where the ball moves within the socket, allowing circular motion in every direction. This is very useful when it comes to having your wheels actually turn.

battery: Like all batteries, the one in your car is a group of two or more cells connected together to provide electrical current. In your car, it's the big square thing under the hood, with cables running in and out of it. If it's dead, your car won't start.

brake calipers and pads: Brake pads are often referred to as "friction material" because they use friction to slow and stop your car. The pads are found on the front brakes. Along with the calipers, they work a bit like a bicycle brake—by squeezing the brake rotor (or disc) and slowing down your car. (See the illustration on page 49 for a closer look.)

brake drums and shoes: Brake shoes are found on the rear brakes of your car, and like the pads up front, are used to slow and stop the car. In this case, the friction is created when the shoes expand and press again the interior of the brake drum. (See the illustration on page 49 for a closer look.)

bushing: A bushing is a rubber or plastic washer-like piece that provides cushioning between two moving parts. If it's worn out, your car's likely going to creak.

cabin (or pollen) filter: This is the filter that allows the interior of the car to remain free from pollen and other impurities that enter from outside. Considering that this is where you and your family sit, you might want to keep this in good working order.

camshaft: The camshaft is a rotating shaft with lobes that open valves at the correct times. When this happens, it allows for proper engine operation. When it doesn't, you've got a problem.

carburetor body: The carburetor body is a network of passages that controls the air-fuel ratio under specific engine conditions.

catalytic converter: In these environmentally conscious times, the catalytic converter is one important piece of equipment. It's a device in the exhaust system that oxidizes (combines with oxygen) most harmful emissions from the engine, making them less damaging to the environment.

chassis: The basic frame of a motor vehicle, the chassis includes the engine, wheels and other mechanical parts, but not the body itself.

clutch: In cars with a manual transmission, the clutch is the device that allows the driver to engage and disengage the gears in the engine and transmission. It's operated by that weird little pedal you push with your left foot.

control arms: Control arms are movable levers that form part of your car's suspension system.

CV joint: A CV joint—or constant velocity joint—provides consistent drive shaft speeds regardless of the operating angle of the joint. CV joints are used primarily on the drive shafts of front-wheel-drive vehicles.

cylinder block: This is the main body of the engine…think of it like the engine's backbone. With apologies for stating the somewhat obvious, the cylinder block holds the cylinders, and it's in these cylinders that the explosions that help propel your car forward occur.

diagnostic lights: You know those pretty lights on your dashboard? If you've read your owner's manual, you'll know that they actually mean something when they light up. They can tell you if you're running low on oil or gas, or if there's a problem with your battery. A word to the wise: pay attention when one lights up. It will likely save you money in the long run.

differential: The differential is the part of the transmission (gearbox) that provides power to the rear axles and allows them to rotate at different speeds, as necessary.

dipstick: No, I'm not referring to your husband/wife/son/daughter/best friend. This dipstick is a strip of stiff metal used to check fluid (like oil) levels. Markings on the stick itself will help you know if it's time to top up the fluid in question.

double-wishbone suspension: This is a suspension system with one of its parts shaped like a wishbone. It's not rocket science, people.

dual brake system: A dual brake system uses two mechanisms—one that operates the front brakes and another that operates the ones at the back. It comprises a pump with two pistons and fluid reservoirs to enhance safety.

engine: The propulsion system that causes your vehicle to move forward, which is generally considered to be a good thing.

engine block: This is the main body of the engine, the part that has the pistons, gears, a crankshaft, one or more camshafts and a timing chain or belt.

engine head: The engine head consists of the cylinder head, valves, maybe a camshaft, a fuel injector or a carburetor, as well as spark plugs and different kinds of springs, seals and gaskets.

exhaust system: When it's working, this vital system allows you and your car to proceed quietly down the road. Parts like the muffler, for example, "muffle" the normal engine noise and direct combustion products (like exhaust gases) to the back of the vehicle. If there's a hole somewhere in the system, you'll know it.

fan belt: A fan belt is a tight rubber belt that transfers torque (a force that produces rotation or torsion) from the crankshaft to the shaft of the cooling fan on an engine.

fuel injector: A fuel injector is simply an electronically controlled valve. It's supplied with pressurized fuel by the fuel pump in your car, and it is capable of opening and closing many times per second. When the injector is energized, an electromagnet moves a plunger that opens the valve, allowing the pressurized fuel to squirt out through a tiny nozzle. The nozzle is designed to turn the fuel into as fine a mist as possible so that it can burn easily. The amount of fuel supplied to the engine is determined by the amount of time the fuel injector stays open.

fuses: Nothing tricky here. Just like in your house, your car has fuses to interrupt electrical currents if a circuit is overloaded or a short occurs. Learn how to find them in your car, and how to change them. You don't want to be stuck in the rain without wipers just because a fuse has blown.

gas filter: This is the filter that allows your engine to remain clear of impurities like dirt, rust and carbon that can enter from the gas tank.

global positioning systems (GPS): These complex and expensive systems can pinpoint your location, which is handy if you're lost or in trouble. The GPS receiver checks data from up to six satellites and then calculates the time taken for each satellite signal to reach the GPS receiver. From the difference in times of reception, it determines your location.

hydraulic brake system: Hydraulic brake systems work via an arrangement of pistons and tubing that uses pressure to transmit force from one part to another. When you press down on the brake pedal, you're compressing hydraulic fluid, which pushes out pistons, which in turn push brake friction material into contact with either discs or drums.

MacPherson strut: A shock absorber spring assembly named after Earl S. MacPherson, a former chief engineer at Ford. A key part of your car's suspension system.

mud flaps: Found behind your car's tires, mud flaps are used to catch the mud that splatters the underside of the car while driving. They'll save you some work when it comes to washing the car.

muffler: The muffler is a key part of your exhaust system. It decreases the noise of vehicle operation. If your muffler has a hole in it, your car will likely make odd and potentially embarrassing spluttering noises.

oil filter: A paper and fiber device that filters oil of impurities. You can change it yourself (see page 86)!

oil minder light: This little light on your dashboard will ever-so-helpfully let your know when it's time to change your oil. Pay attention!

oil pan: The oil pan is the lower section of the case that's used as an oil reservoir on internal combustion engines. You'll need to drain it before attempting an oil change (see page 86).

oil pump: An oil pump uses pressure to force oil into the various parts of the engine where lubrication is needed.

piston: A piston is a short cylinder that moves up and down in a cylinder vessel. It's moved by or against fluid pressure.

rack-and-pinion steering system: The rack-and-pinion steering system tightens or loosens the rack adjustment screws for the best possible steering. (**rack:** flat-toothed bar that is moved left or right by rotation of pinion gear – **pinion:** a small cogwheel on a starter motor that engages a larger wheel to rotate the engine flywheel).

radiator cap: The radiator cap seals and pressurizes the cooling system of your vehicle. If your car is overheating, be very careful when removing the radiator cap. It will be hot, and the fluid inside the radiator itself will shoot out as steam once the built-up pressure is reduced.

radiator fan: The radiator fans cools the radiator (pipes and tubes), which transfers heat from inside your car to the outside world.

spark plug: As the name might suggest, a spark plug gives off an electrical arc—or spark—that ignites the air-fuel mixture in the engine cylinder.

stabilizer bars: These metal bars connect the left and right suspension systems at the front or rear of an automobile or a truck. They are used to stabilize the chassis against sway and, as such, are also called anti-roll bars, anti-sway bars, or sway bars.

starter motor: When this electric motor receives power from the battery, it cranks the motor and starts the internal combustion engine.

steel-belted radials: Steel-belted radials are tires that contain horizontal material cords (stripes) from the inside tire wall to the outside tire wall with the tire tread molded on top. The stripes increase the strength of the tire.

steering column: The steering column is an assembly made up of the steering wheel, steering shaft, ignition key mechanism and other connected parts.

steering gear: This gear assembly turns rotary (circular) motion into linear (straight line) left-right motion to help you steer. Very handy.

tachometer: The tachometer is one of the meters visible on your car's dashboard. Because its job is to tell you when to shift from one gear to another (according to the engine's revolutions per minute) it's most useful in cars with manual transmissions.

tailpipe: This metal tubing carries exhaust from your car's muffler to a point at the rear or side of your vehicle, where it can be dispersed into the atmosphere.

tires: Those black things that your car rides around on. Oh, okay. A rubber cushion that fits around a wheel and usually contains compressed air.

tire valve: This little attachment sticks out of your tire's rim. You need to remove it when putting air into your tire, and replace it once you're done. Lose it, and your tire could develop a slow and annoying leak.

transfer case: The transfer case is the part of the transmission (gearbox) that transfers rotary power from the engine to the wheels.

transmission filter: Like the air filter and the oil filter, the transmission filter's main job is to divert impurities, in this case, from the transmission fluid.

valve lash: This fancy term refers to the clearance between movable mechanical parts that happen to be next to one another. It may only be a fraction of an inch, but it's pretty important to maintain if you want your car to keep working.

valves: Inside the engine, the valves open and close to permit flow into and out of the combustion chamber.

wipers: Ah, the small but humble wiper. At its most basic, it can be described as a device designed for wiping water, snow, slush and bird droppings off your windshield. Give it its due, though, and you'll admit that it could very well be the thing that most consistently prevents you from driving off the road. And that's a very good thing.

Resources

There are a number of government agencies and consumer protection organizations that deal specifically with the automotive industry. Here's a quick look at some I find useful.

The United States

The United States Department of Transportation
Use its Web site to find information about state transportation departments, to report vehicle safety problems, or for information that will help you purchase a new or used vehicle.
400 7th Street S.W.
Washington, DC
20590
Phone: (202) 366-4000
Web site: www.dot.gov
Email: dot.comments@ost.dot.gov

The Council of Better Business Bureaus
This is the umbrella organization for the Better Business Bureau (BBB) system. It was founded in 1912 and now has 250,000 local business members worldwide. Check with them

if you have a problem with a garage or dealership, or for more general information about purchasing a car. For an office in your area, check the Web site or your local phone book.
4200 Wilson Blvd., Suite 800
Arlington, VA
22203-1838
Phone: (703) 276-0100
Web site: www.bbb.org

The American Automobile Association (AAA)

This national consumer protection organization offers everything from travel advice and information to a list of AAA–approved garages that can work on your car. Although you'll need to be a member in order to access its excellent roadside assistance program, a lot of good information is available free on the Web site, including where to find your local office.
1000 AAA Drive
Heathrow, FLA
32746-5063
Phone: (407) 444-7000
Web site: www.aaa.com

The National Highway Traffic Safety Administration (NHTSA)

This organization's mission is to "save lives, prevent injuries and reduce traffic-related health care and other economic costs." The Web site offers a host of information on everything from air bags and child safety seats to vehicle and equipment information. Well worth a look.
400 Seventh Street S.W.
Washington, DC
20590
Phone: 1-800-424-9153
Web site: www.nhtsa.dot.gov
Email: webmaster@nhtsa.dot.gov

Carfax

Carfax offers an invaluable resource for buyers and sellers or used cars—a complete vehicle history. Reports can reveal a lot

about the car you're thinking of buying, including its previous use (was this thing a taxi?), accident history, lien activity and more. Carfax works on-line, though, so you'll need a computer to access this information.
10304 Eaton Place, Suite 500
Fairfax, VA
22030-2213
Web site: www.carfax.com

Canada

Transport Canada
This helpful Web site contains a list of regional offices, information on vehicle safety, buying and selling tips, and links to provincial Ministry of Transportation offices.
330 Sparks Street
Ottawa, ON
K1A 0N5
Phone: (613) 990-2309
Web site: www.tc.gc.ca
Email: webfeedback@tc.gc.ca

The Canadian Council of Better Business Bureaus
This is the umbrella organization for the Better Business Bureau (BBB) system. It was founded in 1912 and now has 250,000 local business members worldwide. Check with the council if you have a problem with a garage or dealership, or for more general information about purchasing a car. For an office in your area, check the Web site or your local phone book.
44 Byward Market Square, Suite 220
Ottawa, ON
K1N 7A2
Phone: (613) 789-5151
Web site: www.bbb.org

The Canadian Automobile Association (CAA)
This national consumer protection organization is an advocate for Canada's motoring and traveling public. Like the AAA, its

U.S. counterpart, the CAA offers everything from travel advice and information to a list of CAA–approved garages that can work on your car. Although you'll need to be a member in order to access its excellent roadside assistance program, a lot of good information is available free on the Web site, including where to find your local office.
1145 Hunt Club Road, Suite 200
Ottawa, ON
K1V 0Y3
Phone: (613) 247-0117
Web site: www.caa.ca

The Automobile Protection Association (APA)

The APA is a membership-based non-profit organization dedicated to promoting consumer interests in the marketplace. The association publishes a yearly *Complete Canadian Used Car Guide*, and the Web site is full of useful information on everything from travel tips to ongoing investigations into vehicle defects.
2 Carlton Street, Suite 1319
Toronto, ON
M5B 1J3
Phone: (416) 204-1444
Web site: www.apa.ca
Email: apatoronto@apa.ca
or
292 St. Joseph Blvd. West
Montreal, Quebec
H2V 2N7
Phone: (514) 272-5555
Web site: www.apa.ca
Email: apamontreal@apa.ca

CarProof

CarProof has electronic access to government databases across Canada. This allows the organization to bring car dealers and consumers current data about vehicles that are, or ever were, registered in Canada. If you're thinking of buying a used car, a CarProof report will reveal the car's history, including liens and

repairs. Reports are requested and delivered via email.
Phone: 1-866-543-6669
Web site: www.carproof.com
Email: info@carproof.com

Repair and Maintenance Record

If you've been paying attention for the last 150 pages, you know that regular maintenance is an important way to ensure your car's long-term health, and that you're more than capable of doing some small repairs yourself. Before you go rushing off to your nearest automotive outlet to buy oil filters and windshield washer fluid, consider using the next few pages to help keep you organized. Think about this as a diary. It will come in handy when your mechanic asks when you last changed your oil, or when you want to know if it's time to have your tires rotated. It will also be invaluable if you decide to sell your car. Just think about how happy you'd be if your potential new car's service history was there for the asking!

Date	Repair/Maintenance Performed	Receipts filed

Date	Repair/Maintenance Performed	Receipts filed

Date	Repair/Maintenance Performed	Receipts filed

Index